Speaking Through The Spirit

An Informational Guidebook For Living Holy

F.L. Blackstone

Copyright © 2023
All Rights Reserved.
ISBN: 978-1-917116-22-0

ACKNOWLEDGEMENT

I dedicate this book to the LORD because without him this book would not have been written, it is all about the LORD and not about me, blessed be the name of the LORD.

This book is also dedicated to my brother in Christ Jay, because without God sending me to minister to him, I would not have even known what God had planted in me to minister.

God used him as the catalyst, and inspiration to inspire me to write this book, and because I ministered to him as God told me to, I now know what I am capable of in the LORD, and I can minister to all those he needs me to and know in my heart I am doing it correctly as God taught me and wanted me to do.

I also dedicate this book to my son's Arturo, Tyrone, and Corey Harris, who are the loves of my life. They were there with me in the beginning, through the good and the bad, they endured with me through everything.

And I count it a blessing to have them, my grandchildren, and my great-grandchildren in my life, and have been allowed to have the greatest opportunity to love them all.

I thank God for my brothers and sisters, I love you all because without you I would not be the person I am today, having all of you as my siblings has been a blessing.

I thank God for my parents, who passed on so long ago, all I can say is that I am glad that God used them to create me. They and God are the reason that I am here, and they made it possible for me to be here to write this book.

I love and appreciate you all

(Deut. 32:1) Listen, O you heavens, and I am going to speak; and hear, O earth, the words that come from my mouth.

In this verse God is talking to everybody who's in heaven, he wanted them to hear him, and he's talking to everybody who's on the earth, he wants them all to hear what he has to say when he speaks.

(Deut. 32:2) My heavenly principles will fall like rain; my words will purify like the dew, like small rain drops on the tender herb, and like the showers that purify the grass.

God is saying that his teachings that come from heaven are going to fall in small amounts like the rain that falls from the sky, and again it will fall in great amounts like the rain falls.

It will fall like a powerful shower that will rain down many small drops, but his teachings will come down with power. His teachings will change men and will skillfully pull sin out of them to the extent that it will clean and renew their souls.

In the same way, it will be put in heaven, and will give as well to the soft gentle light that is Jesus Christ. This will happen at the same time his teachings are doing his work in the earth on the inside of mankind it will also be doing his work in the heavens in his son Jesus Christ.

It will in amounts that will be beneficial to all His children be put into full contact with all of them, this means all of his children in heaven and all of his children who are on earth. This also includes Jesus Christ who is also one of his children.

The word contact means that his teachings will come to touch and unite with each and every one of his children, whether they are living in the heavens or whether they are living on the earth, his teachings will unite with them and unite them with Him.

(Deut. 32:3) For this reason I will proclaim the name of the Lord: you are to accept the greatness of our God.

Because of this I am going to publicly declare the name of the Lord: you are supposed to think carefully about the power that comes through our God.

(Deut. 32:4) He is the Rock, his work is perfect: for all his ways are judgment: a God of truth and without iniquity, just and right is he.

He is the foundation, and the gem, the work he does is excellent and outstanding: because all his ways of doing things are wise: a God of what is real, and who does not have sin in him, who is without blame, and who is good.

Contents

ACKNOWLEDGEMENT	3
INTRODUCTION	9
GOD'S NAMES AND WHAT HE DOES	17
GOD NEEDED HIS SPIRIT	28
OUR COMMISSION	33
HONORING HIM	39
IN THE BEGINNING WAS THE WORD	42
ADAM & EVE	46
PLEASING THE LORD	54
DIVINE FAVOR	61
THE COMFORT OF GOD	66
THE HEALING OF GOD	73
THE LOVE OF GOD 1	77
THE LOVE OF GOD 2	82
THE MIND OF WISDOM	89
GOD SEES THE HEART, LOVE	97
WHEN GOD SPEAKS	107
FASTING	113
YOKES	122
THE PROMISES OF GOD	129
ROOTED & GROUNDED	137

SOWING SEEDS	146
THE TWO SEEDS	151
THE HOLY SPIRIT, CHRIST JESUS	155
THE HOLY SPIRIT, AND GOD'S CHILDREN	165
BEING PERFECTED IN THE SPIRIT	169
VENGEANCE BELONGS TO GOD	174
HOLINESS IS A LIFESTYLE	178
FRIENDSHIP	185
NAMES CHANGED	191
BEING FORGIVING, LOVE	198
BRIDLING THE TONGUE	204
HOLY GROUND	209
FAITH	213
DO YOU KNOW WHO YOU ARE? PRAYER	216
JUDGE NOT	225

Introduction

(1 Cor. 2:9) However like it was written, no eye has ever seen, or any ear has ever heard, nor has ever gone into the heart of man, the things that God has gotten ready for those who love him.

It has been written that no eyes have ever seen, and no ears have ever heard of the things that God has prepared for the true children who love him, neither have any of his things ever gone into the heart of an earthly man.

At this point Paul is talking about the fact that the things that God has prepared for his children who are living in the earth have not been seen by natural eyes or heard by natural ears, and none of these things have ever entered into any man's natural heart.

A man's natural eyes, ears, and heart could never comprehend the spiritual things of God. They can only be seen with spiritual eyes, and heard by spiritual ears, and can only be understood by a spiritual heart.

(1 Cor. 2:10) Still God has shown them to us through his spirit: because the spirit searches all things, yes, only the hidden things of God.

But God makes them known to us only by his Holy Spirit working in us: because the Holy Spirit searches out all of the things of God.

And it only looks for the things of God that he keeps hidden, that he keeps secret. It does not look for anything else, it has no interest in anything else other than Gods secret things.

(1 Cor. 2:11) Because what man knows the things of a man, except the heart of man that is inside of him? Still the truth is the things of God no man knows, except the Spirit of God.

This is because the things of an earthly man only a earthly man knows, does he only know the heart that is inside of him? Truly the things that belong to God no earthly man knows, only the Holy Spirit of God knows them.

They do not know them because they are earthly and not spiritual, only one who knows God will be able to get access to the things of God, and earthly men do not know him.

(1 Cor. 2:12) At this time the spirit of the world has not been given to us, only the Spirit that is of God; so, we might know the things that are given freely to us by God.

The true children do not possess the spirit of the world, that is not what God gives us, he only gives us the Holy Spirit that belongs to him, so we can come to know, and understand the things that he freely gives use.

(1 Cor. 2:13) That happens to be the things that we are also talking about, not using the words that man's knowledge teaches, but using the words the Holy Ghost teaches, discovering spiritual things as they are beside the spiritual.

It just so happens that the things we are talking about, we are not using the words that come from earthly man's knowledgeable teachings.

But we use the words that the Holy Ghost educates us in, we find spiritual things because they are alongside the spiritual, the spiritual they are beside is God himself.

All things exist, and all things have been made by his will not our own. When I walk in the Spirit it is done by his will, and when I speak thus saith the Lord it is done by his will. What we speak, and what we communicate it is by his will, when we write a letter or when we speak his truth it is by his will.

Also, a man who is truly walking in the Lord will not lose his mind because Gods word says that he keeps us, and he keeps us in our right minds.

(Phil. 4:7) And the peace of God, that passes all understanding, will keep your hearts and minds through Christ Jesus.

God's peace moves pass all the understanding that man could ever try to have when it comes to God, and it holds onto the hearts, and minds of the children of God through the finished actions of Jesus Christ, he did this when he died on the cross, and his dying on the cross was his finished action.

(2 Tim. 1:7) Because God has not given us the Spirit to be afraid, but a Spirit of power, and love, and a sane mind.

Due to the fact that God has not given us the spirit to be fearful, but he has given us a spirit of strength, and love, and this spirit gives us a spiritually healthy mind.

(Lk. 8:35) At that time they went out to see what had been done; and came to Jesus, and found the man, that the devils had come out of and left behind, and he was sitting at the feet of Jesus, he was clothed, and in his sane mind: and they were not afraid.

Jesus disciples went to find Jesus to see what he had done; and when they came to Jesus, they found the man, who the devils had been cast out of, and who they had left behind, this man was sitting at Jesus feet, he had clothes on, and he was in his right mind: and his disciples were not scared.

The word also says that what is Gods is Gods, and nothing, and no one can separate us from the love of Christ.

(Rom. 8:35) Who will separate us from Christ's love? Will trials, or pains, or mistreatment, or starvation, or no clothing, or danger, or war?

Is there anything or anybody that can take us away from the love of Christ? Will the things we suffer take us away from him? No, there is nothing that can separate us from the love of Christ. When he chooses us nothing and no one can change the choice that he has made.

My writings may not always be written in the way that it is written in the word but if one sits down with their bible, they will find all that I am saying is in the word. I say this because what I speak and what I write is spirit inspired, spirit filled, spirit instructed, and my footsteps are ordered by God.

(Ps. 37:23) The footsteps of a valuable man are conveniently arranged by the LORD: and he delights in his steps.

The path that a worthy man walks has been purposely prepared by the LORD: and the LORD finds enjoyment in his footsteps.

I have been saved for over 40 yrs. and have been studying the word for the whole period of time that I have known him. I am not a babe in Christ, and it is the spirit of the Lord that has inspired me to write this book.

The Lord does not just speak to his people through his written word, if that were the case then as we walk day by day, we would not hear him speaking directly to our minds, telling us along our walk who to minister to, who to bless, who to pray for, who to help receive their healing.

Everything that I do in my life today I call upon the Lord to direct me, he directs me even when I do not ask him to, he is with me always, I can do nothing without him; he is the way, the truth, and the light. The word also says my sheep know my voice.

(Jn. 10:4) And when he sends out his own sheep, he goes out before them, and his sheep follow behind him: because they know his voice.

When Jesus sends his children out, he goes out before they do, he walks in front of them, and his children follow behind him: and they are able to do this because they know his voice.

(Jn. 10:14) I am the excellent shepherd, and I know my sheep, and am known by my sheep.

Jesus is the remarkable shepherd, and he knows his children, and he is known by his children.

(Jn. 10:27) My sheep are able to hear my voice, and I know them, and they follow behind me:

Only Jesus children are able to hear his voice, and they know him, and follow after him, because they will not follow anybody else.

He also said all that my father has given me none have I lost, so we always know him, and he never loses us, and we always cling to him even when one may think they have fallen from grace, because of the Holy Spirit we continue to call on his name.

(Jn. 6:39) And this is the Father's intentions who has sent

me, of all that he has given to me I will not lose any of it, but I will lift it up once more by the final time.

And this is the Father's aim, the Father who has sent me, concerning all that he has assigned to me I am not going to lose any of it, and I will raise it up once again before I return.

When it says that it will be raised up once again, it is saying that everyone the Father has given to him they will finally appear at a period of time, being assigned to a particular purpose, this is the time that Jesus will spiritually raise them up.

They will be spiritually resurrected, and this will be their last time to be spiritually created, man was originally spiritually created, then he spiritually died in the garden. And now because of Jesus death on the cross he can be spiritually created for the second and last time.

(Isa. 9:6) Because to us a child is born, to us a son is given: and the empire will be on his shoulders: and his name will be called marvelous, ambassador, the strong God, the eternal Father, the Prince of Peace.

Consider the fact that a child has been born to us, and a Son of God was given to us: and a government he would carry the responsibility of, and he would be identified as being the one we would admire.

He would be referred to as being a diplomat of the highest ranking, and he would be assigned this position by God, and he would also be known as the strongest God, the constant Father, and the Prince who would be Peaceful.

This verse is saying, for all of mankind's purposes a baby of the living God was birthed into this world, this child was a boy who was born of a mother who was born on the earth, and who had a spiritual union with the heavenly Father.

Because of this union that his parents had this child was able to be spiritually placed in the womb of his mother's body by the heavenly Father, so when she conceived this child, no earthly man had ever touched her, so this child would not have any sin in him when he was born.

The purpose of this being done was so he could be the savior of all mankind, he was the one true male heir of God, this meant he was the only true son of the living God, and his Father presented him as a gift to mankind: and the names he would be called would be wonderful, minister, magnificent God, the everlasting Father, and the Prince of Peace.

(Isa. 9:7) Of the growth of his empire, and his peace there will be no ending of it, on the throne of David, upward over his kingdom, to command it, and to build it with knowledge, and righteousness from this time forward even so for all eternity. The sincerity of the Lord of armies (hosts) will carry it out.

His body of people will increase immensely, and of his peace there will definitely be no end to it, and in his heavenly position that he was put in place in that was the office of the authority that belonged to King David. David's royal power, and authority was God the Father, and this is the same office of authority that was given to this child.

And in his elevated position, over his domain, his desire would be to command his people, and to get his government to be accepted and recognized, and his government would come with wisdom, intelligence, and keen judgment, and it also would come with him doing what was right, and he would do it with moral principles. This would start from this time moving forward, and it would be in effect forever. The love of the Lord and master that we look forward to has chosen to carry this out and complete it.

The ministry that you are now seeing in this book has been set up a bit differently than even I expected, and the servant God showed how to write this book wrote it in the way that God wanted it to be written, in a way that would be pleasing to him.

When Jesus came some expected a soldier on the battlefield with a physical sword in his hand, but what they got was a peaceful man, and a king of a heavenly government, and all he wanted to do was his Father's will.

And that was to fulfill his Father's plans, and his destiny for him, and that was to die on the cross. So, he could shed his blood, and bring salvation to everyone, and through this he was able to reunite man with the heaven's by bringing man back to the Father, and reuniting man with him.

Because of all God has designed for all his children by releasing his word into the atmosphere, I have made the decision to make this printed work ready voluntarily to glorify the excellent King of kings.

And to let it be known what's the source of who he is, and the source of his beginnings, and that he is remarkable in nature, and character. And that he is noble, and glorious, honor, wisdom, glory, and power to the Lord our God.

This was written by the hand of the Holy Ghost to honor the Lord, it is all about the Lord my God who is able to do from the high place according to his power, and authority. Being able to do things in the lives of those who love him and pay attention to all he has to say to them.

Jesus is the word of God, and this makes him the language of God, he also is the spiritual image of God, and he walks in the Spirit of God, and everything that is in God is in him.

GOD'S NAMES AND WHAT HE DOES

(Ex. 6:3) And I showed myself to Abraham, and to Isaac, and to Jacob, using the name God almighty, but by my name Jehovah they did not know me.

God allowed himself to be seen by Abraham, Isaac, and Jacob, and he told them his name was God almighty, but they did not know him by the name Jehovah.

The meaning of the name Jehovah is God almighty, and he is also known by the name "El Shaddai" which also means God almighty.

(Gen. 17:1) And when Abram was 99 yrs. Old, the Lord showed himself to Abram and said to him, I am the Almighty God; walk in front of me, and you are to be extraordinary.

At the age of 99 yrs. Old the LORD appeared to Abram, and said to him, I am the Almighty God: walk before me, and you are to prove that you can be excellent.

(Ex. 3:14) And God said to Moses, I AM WHO I AM: and he said, in this way you will say to the children of Israel, I AM has sent me to you.

When God referred to himself as "I AM" he was telling Moses to tell the children of Israel that at this present time he did live, and he did exist, he wanted him to tell the children of Israel that he was, and is, and that he ever more will be; I believe he wanted Moses to let them know he was real, and he still was after all their days in Egypt.

(Ex. 17:15) And Moses constructed an altar and called its name Jehovah-Nissi.

And Moses built an altar and named it Jehovah-Nissi.

The name Jehovah-Nissi means the Lord is my banner. The word banner here means Moses believed the Lord was the God of his life that represented his true beliefs, and principles, that the Lord was the standard by which he knew he was going to have to live by.

And because of his belief he built an alter to the Lord and called it what he believed the Lord was Jehovah-Nissi, the Lord was his true belief, and principles, he was his banner.

(Jud. 6:24) Then Gideon constructed an altar to the Lord and named it Jehovah-shalom: to this day it is still in Ophrah, and it is of the Abiezrites.

This name Jehovah-shalom means the Lord is peace, the Lord as the means of our peace, and rest. the peace the Lord gives us is quiet, and calm and it does this on the inside of each of us who believe.

And this peace that he gives us is mentally calming, calming the soul. He gives us his peace so he can be a calming influence on the inside of us, he does this because he is our peace.

(1 Sam. 17:45) Then David said to the Philistines, You come to me with a sword, a spear, and a shield; but I come to you in the name of the Lord of armies (hosts), the God of the armies of Israel, who you have challenged.

In this verse David makes it known that he serves the Lord of the armies of heaven, and the God of the armies of Israel. He is also known by the name "Yahweh Sabbaoth" which means the Lord of Hosts, it refers to God's authority over earthly, and Spiritual armies.

David knew him as the Lord who was the commander of the armies of heaven. David knew he served a God of authority, a God who was in charge of the army of armies.

He knew the army God was in charge of, no man's sword, spear or shield could ever defeat, and David knew the Philistines could never defeat him because he knew who he represented on the battlefield that day.

David knew he represented "Yahweh Sabbaoth" the Lord of hosts. The word hosts means multitudes, it also means a great number of persons.

And it also means a considerable assemblage, so our Lord has authority over a considerable assemblage of heavenly beings that make up his heavenly armies, and the Philistines dared to defy him.

(Ex. 31:13) You are to speak to the children of Israel, and say, really my day of rest you will keep; because it is a sign between you and me from the beginning of your generations: so, you may know that I am the Lord who does sanctify you.

His name here is "Yahweh-Maccaddesheem", the Lord your sanctifier, he was their means of sanctification. He also refers to himself as the Lord that the Sabbath belongs to. The word sanctifier means he is the one that made them holy, he is the one who frees from sin.

The Sabbath belongs to him, and he commanded that it be kept, in their actions of keeping the Sabbath it expressed a certain meaning to God that they were obeying his order according to what he willed for them to.

The Sabbath was the day the Lord designated as a day of rest and prayer, a day that was dedicated to worshiping him. In their keeping of this command, they were showing the Lord that they knew that he was their sanctifier, and they knew that he was the one who made them holy and the one who set them free from sin. "Yahweh-Maccaddesheem" the Lord their sanctifier. And in them keeping his command they would be teaching generations that came after them the importance of honoring God, their children, their children's children, and all their descendants.

(Ps. 23:1) The Lord is my shepherd; I will not want anything.

His name in this scripture is "Yahweh Ro'I", the Lord as the shepherd who cares for his people as a shepherd cares for his sheep. He is the shepherd who herds us and seeks us out to gather us all together using his staff.

(Ps. 23:4) Yes, though I walk all the way through the distresses of the gloom that is over us, I will not be afraid of any evil: because you are with me; your rod, and your staff do give me comfort.

Yes, even though I do walk alone through the depression of the evils of darkness, I will not fear any kind of wickedness: and the reason for this is you are with me; your authority and your assistance (rod & staff) they do comfort me.

The first verse tells us of the Lord as our protector (shepherd), and the second verse tells us of his rod, that is his staff, both of them comfort us, they are what a shepherd uses when he has to take care of his sheep.

They are his switches that he uses to administer correction, and assistance, when he physically and spiritually corrects us. So, the shepherd who is Jesus has a rod that he uses for physical, and spiritual punishment, and correction.

The Lord never uses the rod of correction to strike the soul, he uses it to strike the flesh, because when the flesh is struck, and punishment takes place, then the soul will cry out to God for his assistance; this is why he uses his rod, and his staff of correction to punish the flesh, he wants the man inside to cry out, and when he does cry out, then the man's soul will line up with God's will and live.

A shepherd's staff is a stick with a special use and is his emblem of authority that is what our shepherd's staff is for. It is the power, and authority he uses to show us he is the shepherd of our lives, the shepherd who tends to us, he is our protection, and he guards his sheep of who we are.

The shepherd who watches over us, marching on before us to guide us with his staff to green pastures (Ps. 23:2), protecting us from thieves, murders, and liars, who are in place in front of us. "Yahweh Ro'I", the Lord who is our Shepherd.

(Jer. 23:6) In his days Judah will be saved, and Israel will be able to live in safety: and this is his name by which he will be called, THE LORD OUR RIGHTEOUSNESS.

In this verse his name is "Yahweh-Tsidkenu", the Lord who is our righteousness, and he is the Lord as our righteousness. The word Righteousness means he is the Lord who is recognized by the principles that he lives by.

These principles are morality, justice, and virtue, this God of morality belongs to us, "Yahweh-Tsidkenu" the Lord is our righteousness.

And when we believe in him, and when we trust in him, and except his high moral standards, he in turn places those principles inside of us, and we come to be as he is righteous, and that is why he is our righteousness.

(Ezek. 48:35) It was around about 18,000 in measures: and the name of that city from that day on will be, the Lord is there.

In this verse Ezekiel is talking about the dimensions of a structure that was like a city, and in that city was a temple that he was able to describe the dimensions of. And the name of that city was, the Lord is there.

In this verse his name is "Yahweh-Shammah", the Lord is there, and the Lord was there then, and he is here for us now.

(1 Jn. 5:7) Consider the fact that there are three who make up the record of their history that is in heaven, the Father, the Word, and the Holy Spirit: and the three of them are one.

This verse is saying to think about the fact that in heaven there are three that make up the record of their past events in heaven. These three are the Father, the Word, and the Holy Spirit. They are also referred to as the Father, the Son, and the Holy Spirit.

In this verse he is known as just "Yahweh", the Lord God of Israel. He is also called "Elohim" which is the plural of majesty and refers to the trinity.

El in his name means strong one, he is the strong Majesty, who is the Father, Son, and the Holy Spirit, these three are the trinity spoken of above in this verse.

(Dan. 7:22) Till the Ancient of days came, and judgment was bestowed to the saints of the most high; and the time came when the saints had the kingdom.

Until the God who lived in the far past who was of the generations came, and decision making was given to the children of the Most High God; and the time did come when the children of God were given the kingdom and we are a part of those children.

In this verse his name is "El-Elyon" this name refers to his strength, kingship, and his supreme power. By the name "El-Olam" he is known as the everlasting God.

Also, the word ancient in this scripture means that he has existed since the time of legal memory, and of days means he is of the light, so he is the light who lived in times past, or you can call it times of old, and his existence first began a very long time ago.

The God who lived in the far past who was of the generations was the LORD GOD Almighty, he was of the entire body of those who were spiritually alive, and who believed in him, and he was the one who gave us the right to choose to live righteous, or to choose to be in unrighteousness.

Before he came all we knew was sin, and before he died, we had no choice, for us he made all things possible. And because of his sacrifice Gods kingdom was finally able to be given to us as a gift.

(1 Tim. 4:10) Since then we both work and endure painful disgrace, for this reason we trust in the living God, this person who is the Savior of all men, particularly the Savior of those who believe.

Now then we both labor, and bear painful shame, and because we have learned how to trust in the God who is alive, this God who we believe in is the God who died on the cross, and became the Savior of all men, precisely he is the Savior of everyone who believes.

In this verse the Lord is the living God, and Savior. In

(Duet. 10:17) he is our Lord who is Lord of Lord's, Jesus Christ.

(Duet. 10:17) Because the Lord your God is the God of gods, and he is the LORD of lords, and an important God, a strong, and a frightful God, who does not honor anybody, and does not take awards:

The LORD our God is the one true God over any other God that men may want to worship, and he is the ultimate LORD, there are no other lords out there that are like him, he is the only one that matters, he is mighty, and to be feared, he pays no respect to any man, and he can't be bribed.

(Ex. 24:17) And seeing the glory of the Lord was similar to a hungry flame on the top of the mountain in the sight of the children of Israel.

And glimpsing the glory of the LORD was like a flame that was consuming the top of the mountain in the children of Israel's eye's..

In this verse he is the "Lord of glory", his glory was a sight the children of Israel where able to see with their own eyes, and he burned like embers on the top of his mountain in front of them.

They were given a view of him and were able to carefully watch him, and what they saw was his glory, his brilliant beauty, and they saw how his appearance was so impressive. They saw him even though he was in the form of a consuming, living, bright flame.

As he remained attached to the highest point of the mountain. They saw him like this because God allowed them to see him in this way; they saw him as he wanted them to see him, and when they looked, they saw the Lord of glory, as his glory.

(Matt. 7:7-11) These verses tells us, he is a "provisional God", who gives good gifts, and the word provision means he is a God who supplies all our needs, he prepared this arrangement for us before any of us were even born.

And all we have to do is seek him so we can ask of him, this is one of the conditions of his provisions, all we have to do is look for him and he will provide for us.

(Ezek. 34:30) So, will they know that I the LORD their God am with them, and they who are of the house of Israel, are my people, said the LORD God.

Then, they will know I the LORD their God am with them, and those who are of the house of Israel, who are my people, the LORD God said.

(Acts 2:23) He, in actuality was turned over to you through certain council, and the foresight of God, and you have taken him, and by evil hands have hung him on the cross, and killed him:

He, actually was turned over to you through a specific council, through the foreknowledge of God, and you took him, and through evil hands you hung him on the cross, and murdered him:

Jesus was put in the hands of those who would kill him through the evil council they took up against him, they assembled together and discussed it and decided to kill him. And God already knew they would do this because he had foreknowledge of what they were going to do.

He is a God of foreknowledge, and the word foreknowledge means he has the knowledge of what is going to happen before it does.

So, he is able to instruct us in matters before they even happen because he has seen the conclusion of it and He knows the outcome of it. Jesus being hung on the cross was done because it was something God definitely said would happen, and it was spoken of through the prophets.

(Rom. 10:9) So, if you will acknowledge with your mouth the Lord Jesus, and will believe in your heart that God has raised him up from the dead, you will be saved.

If you will speak the truth with your mouth about the Lord Jesus Christ and are willing to believe in your heart that God did raise him up from the dead, you will be delivered from the power, and the penalty of sin.

(Heb. 12:6) Because who the Lord loves he chastises, and he scourges every son who he receives.

For whom the Lord loves he corrects, and spiritually whips every son that he receives.

God is a God of correction; he corrects us by allowing afflictions and suffering to be inflicted on us for the purpose of making us spiritually change. When we spiritually change, we become what God wants us to be, and we become spiritually better on the inside. And the purpose of this is so we will improve morally on the inside, through him teaching us how to be humble.

The word scourge means to inflict punishment or correction. Back in the disciples' times people were punished by being scourged, and the word scourge also means to whip.

Jesus was whipped, and we are not better than him, and because he was whipped it is by his stripes that we were healed.

God loves us so much, and that is why he spiritually corrects us, and the spiritual correction that we receive is done to all the children he takes ownership of.

It is done to every child that offer's themselves to him, and by doing this he saves the soul of the believer, and makes their flesh behave so the spirit man can live and be of use to him.

God Needed His Spirit

God needed his Spirit to write the book "Speaking through the Spirit" because there are many souls out in the world that do not understand the Bible, and who do not even know that it is the word of God.

People who want to read it and can't, or who want to be taught and do not have the proper teachers to teach them, or who do not know how to call on God to give them the knowledge to read his book.

There's so much sin in some churches today, and those running it, because they are too busy walking after their own sinful ways.

Not being able to teach those they call their congregation but are draining them dry of the money that is in their pockets, because that is really their major concern to run the church like a business, and not as the house of God it is supposed to be.

So many people want to know what God really has to say in his word, and they want to know what is required of them, and they are not able to find out because there are so very few teacher's out there who can guide them in the right direction.

And there are many people in the world today who just don't want to go to church or hear anything about God, because many think churches are full of people who are fake and fraudulent, and many are tired of being lied to.

And others have been terribly hurt because of how they were treated when they went to church by people who said they served the Lord, but their behaviors told a different story. Basically, they did not treat them like they were people who knew God.

(Matt. 9:37) Jesus said to his disciples; that the season of maturity is here, it is time to gather and store, the supply being fruitful and abundant, but the required workers are in limited supply, so you could say there isn't enough of them.

This verse is saying that the season of the maturity of the Holy Spirit had come because Jesus came, so it was time to gather God's people. It was time to gather those who would receive the Holy Spirit after Jesus death, and after he released his Holy Spirit into his Father's children over time, and down through time. The only problem was God needed workers, faithful children who would do the work from a good heart, but in those days, there were hardly any.

(Matt. 9:38) You are to pray then that the LORD of the harvest will send out workers into the harvest.

Then he tells them that they are to pray, and ask the LORD, and give thanks to God for the reason that he has set aside this time period. And this is the time that he has chosen to give the order to make the workers that are needed to be able to go out at this time.

He would lead them, and bring them to his things, and he would allow them to enter into the things that belonged to him, in his period of time.

So, Jesus told them that the time had come to get the work done, the fruit of the spirit was here inside of him. So, he told the disciples to talk to the Father, and ask of him, and show him the highest respect, and thank him for what they knew he was going to do.

So, the Father would decide to send out the command to call the workers, and give them directions, making them come. Everyone who belonged to the LORD, on that day, and down through time.

They would be made to come to his courts and come before his throne to do the work for him he needed them to do, he needed them to gather his people, the children of God.

When God made the decision to do this, and the workers came he would bring them to his Holy Spirit, and by him introducing them to the Holy Spirit he would be giving them entry into what belonged to him.

He would give them entry into his holy things, but they would enter in only in his time. These workers that he would allow in would be the only ones who had access to what he wanted them to have and wanted them to learn.

If he does not give you entry then you can't enter in, and if he does not call you teacher, and give you his teaching tool, the Holy Ghost then you can't learn, and you can't teach. There are many people who call themselves teachers but are not, many call themselves teachers when God has not called them to be teachers.

They are self-appointed teachers who walk after the flesh, and the spirit is not in them. They can't bring the harvest in because they don't possess inside of themselves the true reaper of the harvest, the Holy Ghost. Flesh can't do anything of itself for God; the Holy Ghost does everything for him, and for us.

If anyone goes out trying to preach and teach the word of God when God has not given the command for them to do it, their work will be done wrong, it will be done in vain, and God will not get the glory for what they themselves have chosen to do.

And their effort will be evil spoken of because it was done in self, and not in the will of the Lord. And what they have been doing that is wrong will eventually be judged by God in front of men, and the fall of that person will not be pretty.

This word was written through the power, and authority of God, he gave the order to my soul threw his Holy Ghost for this book to be written. He is saying the harvest has matured, and ripened, and it is ready for the workers to come and cut down sin.

By allowing his Holy Ghost to use them to gather his people and bring them to him. But because there are so few laborers the harvest isn't being brought in.

When God summons us to come to him, he puts an order on our lives, he says I want you to serve me, and if you do as I ask then in return for your obedience, I will give you all that I have promised in my word. And because I am in your life, I will make you and your life all that I can make it, and more than you could ever expect it to be. But if you choose not to serve me, I will do in your life all I have promised to one who is disobedient, the choice is yours.

All on this earth have the right to choose, but if some are not properly informed by one who says call me teacher, then the right to choose was never put in their hands, and this so-called teacher is not leading to righteousness but to unrighteousness.

It is not good for a people to be made to remain ignorant, and blind just because someone loves money, and earthly possessions more than God, and his righteousness, and chooses to lie, and miss lead, and call themselves a teacher. AMEN!!!

OUR COMMISSION

(Matt. 28:18) And Jesus came and spoke to them saying, authority has been given to me in heaven and earth.

Jesus came to them and said everything of power has been placed in my hands, and is now under my control, I am able to influence thoughts, behaviors, and governments, and I have control over everything in heaven, and on earth, I have been given this position, it was a gift to me, and I am sitting in that position right now.

(Matt. 28:19) You go then, and teach all people, baptizing them in the name of the Father, Son, and Holy Ghost.

You are to go make followers of me of those who come from all kingdoms, lands, and governments. And You are to baptize them in the name of the Father, the Son, and the Holy Spirit.

(Matt. 28:20) Teaching them to notice all things whatever I have instructed you: and look, I am with you at all times, even to the end of the world. Amen.

Teaching wisdom to them and instructing them to behave in agreement with all I have taught you. And look, without fail I am with you always, only until the ending of the world. So Be It.

(Mk. 16:15) And he said to them, you are to go into all the world, and proclaim the gospel to all creation.

And he told them to move forward and go out into the farthest parts of the world to all mankind, and make known the good knowledge of the word, to all creation, that means it is to be made known to everything and everybody in the world that God made.

(Mk. 16:16) He who believes and is baptized will be saved; but he who does not believe will be condemned.

Anyone that understands, and is immersed in water (baptized), and are dedicated to the Father they surely are to be rescued, protected, and kept (saved).

From another point of view, anyone whose actions are to deny this knowledge, and refuse to understand the word of God, they are to surely be declared unfit for Gods service, and it will be announced that they are guilty and sentenced to be punished.

(Mk. 16:17) And these signs will follow those who believe; in my name they will reject devils; and they will speak with a new way of talking.

These are the events that will follow those who have faith in Jesus' name, they will be able to refuse demons; and they will also be able to talk with a new way of talking.

Their way of talking will change once they start believing in Jesus and change once they receive the gift of the Holy Spirit, because they have been changed on the inside, and the Holy Spirit becomes their voice.

(Mk. 16:18) They will tackle demons; and if they consume any destructive thing, it will not hurt them; they will place their hands on anyone who is sick, and they will regain their health.

Those who believe in Jesus will deal with the problem of Demons; and if they should destroy any destructive thing, it will not hurt them. And they will position their hands on any person who is spiritually ill, and the spiritually ill person will recover from their illness. Back in the disciples days there were some whose physical bodies recovered, and then there were some whose souls recovered.

When it says if they should destroy any destructive thing this means should they spiritually put an end to anything that spiritually tries to destroy them or anyone who is around them using the word of God.

It will be unable to do any harm to them because it can't, because the word is their protector, and it will protect them. And it says in the word resist the Devil and he will run; it does not say that he will attack.

(Jn. 21:15) Then when they had eaten, Jesus said to Simon Peter, Simon, son of Jonas, do you love me more than the others? He said to him, Yes, Lord, you know that I love you. He said to him feed my sheep.

They had just finished eating when Jesus asked Simon Peter did, he love him? and was he devoted to him to a greater degree than the other disciples?

When he asked him, this Jesus was pointing out the difference between Peter and the other disciples who were sitting with them that day, he was using a comparison when he asked him did, he love him more than the others?

He was making it known to Peter how great a love he had inside of himself for him, and he wanted him to use that love to nurture, support and encourage his meek, timid, and spiritually unimaginative children who were out in the world.

Those who needed what Jesus was carrying inside of himself, they needed what was going to be put inside of Peter, the Holy Spirit.

And it would provide for them what was necessary for

them to spiritually live and grow, and it would help them in their spiritual development in spiritual matters, it was what would bring them to the knowledge of Jesus Christ and his Father.

(Jn. 21:16) He said it to him again a second time, Simon, son of Jonas, do you love me? He said to him, Yes, Lord; you know that I love you. He said to him, Feed my sheep.

Jesus asked him for a 2nd time, Peter do you really love me? Do you sincerely worship me? Peter answered yes Lord you know all that is right in me, you know I love you, and again Jesus told him to teach his children.

(Jn. 21:17) He said to him a third time, Simon, son of Jonas, do you love me? Peter was in pain because he said this to him a third time, Do you love me? And he said to him, Lord, you know all things; you know that I love you. Jesus said to him, Feed my sheep.

Then Jesus asked him a 3rd time, Peter do you really love me? Peter was upset because of this question, he was upset because Jesus asked him a 3rd time was he devoted to him, again Peter responded to Jesus you understand completely all thoughts, and you know I love you. Then he told him again to teach his children (sheep) and feed them his spiritual food.

Jesus used Peter as an example so that the other disciples could see his love, and devotion for him, Peter did not understand what Jesus was doing, and that is why he was upset, he thought Jesus was questioning his love for him, but he was not, he wanted the others to see Peter's love for him.

We were given an order to do the will of the Lord; we were given the power to make followers of all nations, to preach, and to teach the children who are Jesus' sheep the knowledge of God. And we are to baptize them in the name of the Father, the Son, and the Holy Spirit.

We are to do all the things Jesus has ordered us to do, we were even given the power to be able to forgive those who sin against us, and only by the Holy Spirit can this truly be done; we are able to be a forgiving people because we have chosen to follow the example of our Lord, and Savior Jesus Christ, and we are able to do this because of the Holy Spirit that is inside of all the children of God.

(Jn. 21:18) Really, really, I say to you, When you were young, you girded yourself, and walked where you would: but when you get older, you will stretch out your hands, and another will gird you, and carry you wherever you would not go.

Then Jesus told them actually, I am saying to you that when you were in your youth, you braced yourself, and you walked were you wanted to walk but when you get older, you will extend your hands, and someone else will brace you, and take you wherever you would not go.

This is saying in their youth before they came to know Jesus they walked and went wherever they wanted to go. They would get themselves ready to walk, without the help of God, young people tend to have an "I can do anything" frame of mind, and they do not think about what they are going to do when they do it.

But when we get older, we get cautious, and the things we did in our youth we don't even think about doing in our older age. He was letting them know that in their later years the Holy Spirit would be there with them.

And when they stretched out their hands to do the work Jesus, and his Father wanted them to do it would be the Holy Spirit that would brace them and take them wherever they would not go on their own, and it did.

When we do as he has so ordered us to do, we are showing him how much we love him, and how important doing the work for his kingdom is, and how important he is in our lives.

We are being obedient sons and daughters of the Most High God, and we are showing Jesus, and other's that our love for him is the same love that Peter had for him as well.

Honoring Him

(Isa. 43:7) In fact everyone who is called in my name: Are called because I have made him for my glory. I have formed him; yes, I have made him.

In this verse the word called means that he is going to make contact with everyone through the use of his name to get them to come to him: his name has the power to make contact with us, his name has its own voice, it is on a regular basis heard by those that can hear his name coming out of the spiritual realm..

These people who can hear it have been made to tune into the sound of this name in the spiritual realm. He is able to make contact with them because it was him who made them with the purpose of them praising, and worshiping him,

(Rev. 2:7) He who has an ear allow him to hear what the holy spirit says to the churches.

This verse is saying that only those who have been given a spiritual ear to hear the spirit will hear what the spirit is saying to them, and the churches are those who are his chosen people, the churches that were set up in the New Testament, and the future chosen people of God.

You can only have an ear to hear if God has given it to you, and it is the name of Jesus itself that makes contact with us. This name has an authoritative command over our souls, this name is authorized, and ordered to gather together the children of God, calling us to the duty of his Father.

This name has the authority to call us from the ends of the earth, and from the pits of a life that is hell on earth. This name has the power to call our souls into action for our Father, and this name has the power to raise us up from a spiritual sleep should the Lord have need of thee. This name was given all power, and all authority in heaven and earth.

This name God uses to make us so we can glorify him, this name God used to create the angles of heaven. This name he used to form us, the wonderful name of Jesus. This name summons us to his kingdom, and into his courts, to bask in his Glory, and to honor him.

We are to honor him so he will be enlarged in our lives, the word enlarge means that when we speak of him, his power grows larger in our lives, this happens when we acknowledge his Kingship, and when we acknowledge him before all mankind, the one who carries this name, and this power is the Alfa and the Omega, the Beginning, and the End. He is the author, and the finisher of our faith, and his name is Jesus.

We are to honor him with all that we are, and with all that we do, with every move we make, and every breath that we take. We are to honor him with our words, our souls, and with the songs from our hearts, honor him with our time, and our money.

We are to honor him in the dance, and in the praise, we are to honor him in true humility, and in prayer, we are to honor him in sorrow, and in joy, we are to honor him because he is our God.

To honor God is to worship him by the spirit, and it is to adhere to a strict conformity to what is considered morally right, and due to God, it is owed to him, and it is because of this spirit that we are able to honor him.

To honor him is to show integrity, and integrity is a soundness of moral principles that no power or influence on earth can corrupt, walking upright in Gods righteousness before him. When we walk like this before him it pleases him and makes him happy.

(Ps. 147:11) The Lord takes pleasure in those who fear him, in those who hope in his goodwill.

This verse is saying, the Lord gets joy, having such a feeling of delight so deep, and so lasting that it radiates happiness, and radiates his glory.

And this radiation comes because of his chosen who respect him, and reverence him, seeing that he is a God to be revered with awe, and he gets joy in those that believe in him, desire him, rely on him, and trust in his kindness, his compassion, and his divine favor.

The God that we serve is a good God, honor him, he is a loving God, honor him, he is the compassionate God, honor him, he is a faithful God, honor him, he is the true God, honor him, and he will respect your sacrifices, and honor your sacrifices of praise.

IN THE BEGINNING WAS THE WORD

(Jn. 1:1) That from the start of everything Jesus Christ existed in the heaven's, he was with God, and he was God.

This same Jesus was there from the beginning of everything, and he was there with God, because he was God.

(Jn. 1:2) This same person was with God in the beginning.

This is the same Jesus who was with God from the very beginning.

(Jn. 1:3) Everything that was made was made through him; and without him not one thing was made that was created.

Everything that is, was created through the authority of Jesus Christ, and had he not existed nothing would have been made.

(Jn. 1:4) In him there was life; and this life was the light that belongs to all men.

Inside of Jesus was a spiritual life, and this life was something that was the spiritual light of all men, and this light belonged to every man, this light was the holy spirit.

(Jn. 1:5) And this Light shinned in the darkness; and the darkness did not understand it.

This spiritual light would shine in the dark, and the dark would not understand it, or receive it.

From the beginning of Genesis, and before the worlds were formed the Word was with God because the Word was God, and who is the Word, Jesus Christ. How is this possible?

The word is a spirit as God is a spirit, and until the Word was made flesh, and put down here to live among men, he like everything and everybody else lived in God by the spirit.

God created all things through Jesus, the heavens and the Earth, animals, me, and you, and without him nothing would have been made.

All was created through him because he was the light of all men and Satan was the darkness of all men. The darkness whether it was the darkness of men, or Satan, are not able to understand the light of God, and the holy spirit is that light.

I believe God knew he was going to have Satan become evil before he founded the earth, and prior to his becoming evil God already had Jesus with him, he had the light with him because the light was him.

I believe God made Satan the adversary because he knew when he created man, he was going to have to create a way to make man's road hard because he already knew man was going to be a stubborn and disobedient creature.

He knew because he had already planned to make man this way, to me if a God was going to set all things up in the way he did he would have already had to have had the light to fight the darkness before he created the darkness.

And I believe he would have created the darkness because he already knew it was going to be something necessary to help direct man into the direction, he wanted him to walk to fulfill what he had already mapped out for him from the very beginning. And if any man should think that God works by coincidence, they are sadly mistaken, he does not work that way, he had everything planned from the very beginning. He can see over thousands of years down the road to what he wants done in this world in the future, and what he wants done in the lives of the children of men, he sees everything.

(Ex. 3:13) And Moses said to God, Look, when I come to the children of Israel, what will I say to them, The God of your fathers has sent me to you; and they will say to me, What is his name? what will I say to them?

Moses said to God, when he went to the children of Israel, he was to tell them the God of your fathers has sent me to you; and they will say to him, What is his name? what am I to say to them?

(Ex. 3:14) And God said to Moses, I AM WHO I AM: and he said, In this way you will say to the children of Israel, I AM has sent me to you.

Then God said to Moses, I AM THE ONE THAT I AM: and he said, In this way you will say to the children of Israel, I AM THE ONE THAT I AM. He was telling Moses who he was, the one and only God of Israel.

(Ex. 3:15) And God said furthermore to Moses, in this way you will say to the children of Israel, the LORD of your fathers, the God of Abraham, the God of Isaac, and the God of Jacob, has sent me to you: this is my name eternally, and this is my memorial to every generation.

God told Moses as well, that he was to tell the children of Israel in a certain way that the LORD of their fathers, the God of Abraham, Isaac, and Jacob, had sent him to them: and the name that Moses was to say to them was the name he would have forever, and this name was a memorial to all their descendants.

(Jn. 8:58) Jesus said to them, Really, really, I say to you, Before Abraham was I am.

Jesus said to them, truly, truly, I'm saying to you, that before Abraham had ever been born, I was alive.

This verse is how we know Jesus was God because in Exodus God told Moses to tell the Israelites "I AM" sent him, and Jesus called himself the same name years after the Exodus of the children of Israel out of Egypt.

(Gen. 1:26) And God said, Let's make man in our form, after our appearance: and let them have command over the fish of the sea, and the fowl of the air, and over the cattle, and over all the earth, and over every crawling thing that crawls on the earth.

God said, let's make man in our image, and our nature: and let them be allowed to have control over the fish, and the birds that fly, and the cattle, and all of the earth, and over all that crawls on the ground.

From this scripture it states God said let us make man in our form, so again this scripture lets us know God made man with someone else.

Adam & Eve

(Gen. 2:18) And the LORD God said, it's not good for the man to be alone; I will make him a helper who is fit for him.

The LORD God said that it was not good for the man to be by his self; so, he decided to make a companion that was suitable for him.

(Gen. 2:21) And the LORD made a deep sleep fall on Adam, and he fell asleep: and he removed one of his ribs, and then he closed up the flesh of it instantly.

Then the LORD in a special way caused a heavy sleep to come down on Adam, and he went to sleep, then God took out one of his ribs, then he closed up the flesh of Adam's body immediately.

(Gen. 2:22) And the rib, that the LORD God took from the man, he made a woman from it, then he brought her to the man.

And the rib, the LORD God removed from the man, he made a woman out of it, and then he delivered the woman to the man.

(Gen. 2:23) And Adam said, this is now bone of my bone, and flesh of my flesh: she will be called woman, do to the fact that she was taken out of man.

Then Adam said at this moment this is bone of my bone, and flesh of my flesh: and she will be called woman, because she was taken out of man.

He did not tell Adam to go out, and find a woman, he said

he would create a woman for him. It is not good for a man to be alone because alone a man can get into all kinds of trouble, and even get into things that are not what God meant for him to get into. Besides alone man gets lonely, and he begins to cry in his heart for companionship.

I believe God knew this would happen so he took care of the problem before man could even begin to cry for what at that time, he did not even know he would be crying for. The woman had not been taken out of the man at the time God said it is not good for man to be alone.

I was sitting and wonder what it was like for Eve knowing she was created through God putting Adam to sleep, and taking a rib out of him, and forming it into her (if she knew at all), being made not just directly from him, but being made just for him.

(Gen. 2:25) And both of them were nude, the man, and his wife, and they were not embarrassed.

And the two of them together were naked, the man, and his wife, and they were not ashamed.

They were not ashamed before their fall because they knew each other as God had wanted them to, as husband and wife, and at the time they still had their communication with God. Their shame came from being naked in front of God after they had sinned, after they ate the fruit of the tree God told them not to eat of.

(Gen. 3:6) And when the woman saw the tree was good to eat, and it was pleasing to the eyes, and a tree that should be desired to make one wise, she did take of the fruit then, and she did eat it, and then she gave as well to her husband with her; and he ate it.

But when the woman laid her eyes on the tree, she saw that

the tree was able to be eaten, and it was a pleasure to look at, and that it was a tree to crave to make one smart, she took a piece of the fruit, and she ate it, and then she also gave a piece to her husband, and the two of them did eat it.

(Gen. 3:7) And their eyes were opened, and they became mindful that they were nude; and they sewed fig leaves together and made aprons for themselves.

Then their eyes opened up, and they became aware of the fact that they were naked; then they stitched fig leaves together and made coverings for themselves.

When I read this verse, I thought how did they know how to sew fig leaves together? How they knew was because they gained the knowledge when they ate of the tree.

Just like them coming to know that they were nude, and coming to know good, and evil. When their eyes opened it was the eyes of the flesh that opened, and their spiritual eyes closed on that day because their spiritual existence died when they ate that fruit.

(Gen. 3:8) Then they heard the LORD God's voice walking in the garden in the cool of the day: then Adam and his wife concealed themselves from the spirit of the LORD God among the trees in the garden.

Then they were able to hear the LORD's voice moving in the garden in the cool of the day: and at that time Adam, and his wife hid themselves from the LORD God's spirit, hiding in the midst of the trees in the garden.

(Gen. 3:9) And the LORD God called to Adam, and said to him, Where are you?

Then the LORD called out to Adam, saying to him where

are you?

(Gen. 3:10) And he said, I could hear your voice in the garden, and I was afraid, due to the fact that I was nude; and I hid myself.

Then Adam said to the LORD, I heard your voice in the garden, and I got scared. Because I was naked; and I hid myself.

(Gen. 2:11) Then he said, Who told you that you were nude? Have you eaten of the tree, of which I ordered you that you should not eat?

Then the LORD said, who told you, you were naked? Have you eaten from the tree, that I told you, you were not to eat?

When he told them not to eat, he did not mean by opening their mouths, he meant do not spiritually eat it, basically he was telling them not to believe in it, he did not want them to spiritually eat the fruit of that tree, and they ended up eating it anyway.

When they ate of the tree they had no tongues, they did not have tongues until their bodies were changed by sin and they were turned into flesh that had sin in it.

And after their fall they were separated from God, and God bound them to one another according to the punishment he spoke over them. When we eat something, we eat it because we believe it is going to taste good, and this is what they did, they believed in it.

(Gen. 3:12) And the man said, the woman that you gave to be with me, she gave to me from the tree, and I did eat it.

The man said, the woman you gave to be with me, she gave the fruit from the tree to me, and I did eat it.

(Gen. 3:16) To the woman he said, I will to a great degree

increase your anguish and your fertility; in anguish you will bring forth children; and will crave your husband, and he will have control over you.

The LORD said about Eve, I will greatly boost in a series of stages your pain, and your reproduction; in pain you will bring children forth; and you will need your husband, and he will completely dominate you.

I thought about it when he said in a series of stages, he was going to boost her pain, the word boost means he was going to raise her pain and her pregnancy rate.

If you think about it woman have pain when giving birth, we go through pain when raising our children when they are rebellious or disrespectful.

We go through pain when we find out our children are suffering or when we find out our underage child is going to have a baby, we go through pain when a child dies that we gave birth to.

We go through a lot of pain to bring our children into this world, and to raise them, and for those who choose to have many children their pain is double or more. Yes, he greatly increased her pain and the pain of every woman who came after her, this was the penalty of her sin.

You could also say that the pains that women suffer was given to them in stages, each thing that a woman suffers is a new stage in their lives, and the word series also means events. So, each thing that a woman suffers would be another event in her life.

(Gen. 3:17) And to Adam he said, due to the fact that you have obeyed the voice of your wife, and have eaten of the tree, of which I ordered you, saying, You shall not eat of it the whole entire days of your life.

Then God said to Adam, because you complied with the voice of your wife, and ate the fruit of the tree, that I told you not to eat, telling you, you should not eat of it all the days of your life;

(Gen. 3:18) Then briars and prickly plants it will bring forth to you; and you will consume the herb of the field.

Thorny twigs, and troublesome plants the earth will cause to grow out for you; and you will eat the plants of the ground.

(Gen. 3:19) In the sweat of your face will you eat bread, till you return to the ground; because out of it were you taken; because dust you are, and to dust you will return.

With your face covered in sweat you will eat bread, until you go back to the ground; because you were brought forth from the earth; because you are dust, and back to the dust you will go.

Their sins destroyed their quality of life because it caused them to die the minute they took the fruit into their spiritual bodies, they were not supposed to eat, and Adam placed the blame on God saying: "the woman you gave to be with me." Yes I will just shift the blame on to God; he was wrong for that.

(Gen. 3:21) To Adam as well and his wife the LORD God did make coats of skins and clothed them.

For Adam, and his wife the LORD God made them clothes of skins to cover their nakedness.

(Gen. 3:22) And the LORD God said, Look, the man has come to be one of us, to know good and evil: and at this time should he put out his hand, and also take of the tree of life, and does eat, he will live eternally:

Then the LORD God said, pay attention, the man is now like one of us, he now knows good and evil: and now should he raise his hand, and take from the tree of life, and eats it, he will live forever:

After they sinned God was concerned that they would touch the tree of life, and had they then Adam & Eve would have lived forever in the sinful condition they were in. Man was made in their image, but he was not like them when he was made, he did not know good, and evil like God, and Jesus did.

(Gen. 3:23) As a result the LORD God sent him at once from the garden of Eden, to plow the ground from where he was taken.

Because of what they did the LORD God sent him right away out of the Garden of Eden, to till the soil that he had been brought forth out of. This verse says the LORD sent him right away out of the garden.

It does not say him and her, this is because the two were considered to be one man, so only the man was mentioned as being thrown out. And it was the man who was told that he would work the ground from where he was taken, not the woman.

In (Gen. 3:16) Eve was told her sorrows, and conception would be greatly multiplied, and some might think this was a total punishment, but it was not, it was a precaution.

By placing this commandment on her life that she would desire her husband God created a way to make sure she bore children to Adam, God created a way to make sure they would be fruitful and multiply.

A way to make sure her sorrow was multiplied, and her conception was too, but it was also a way for them to have a fleshly closeness, a type of union to make the two as one, and the two would be one in the children they had. God created something between them that would make Eve be submissive to Adam.

She had to learn how to allow her husband to have rule over her like her punishment was spoken over her. God knew what she was capable of because of what she did in the garden, and if she was allowed to do what she wanted without putting Adam as ruler over her, God knew what could happen.

In making Adam rule her God forced Adam to take his position over his wife. God made Adam the head, and he was not about to allow Eve to lead, he did not give the position to her, he gave it to Adam. This would also teach Eve how to be humble and submissive to her husband.

Pleasing the Lord

(Prov. 16:6) Through kindness and truth sin is purified: and through the fear of the LORD men leave evil behind.

Through kind behavior, and truth sin is cleaned: and through fearing the LORD men stop following after sin.

(Prov. 16:7) When a man's actions, please the LORD, he makes even his adversaries to be at peace with him.

When a man's direction in life is pleasing to the Lord, the Lord will make even those who are nasty to him, who are his enemies to be at peace with him.

(Lam. 3:25) The LORD is good to those who wait on him, and to the soul who searches him out.

The LORD is wonderful to those who wait for him, and to the person who seeks him out.

(Lam. 3:26) It is right for a man to believe, and at the same time humbly wait in patience for the LORD to come and deliver him.

In righteousness it is a wonderful thing when a man looks forward in expectation, looking for the source, by whom we are saved, and delivered from the power, and the penalty of sin, and that source is the LORD GOD Almighty.

(Lam. 3:27) It is good for a man to hold up under the burdens he experiences in his childhood.

It is beneficial for a man to hold up under the pressures of being young, and inexperienced.

It is good for a man when he is young to learn how to stand up under the hardships and the pressures that they must go through, because these things teach them the experience that they need to learn to get through the things they must suffer in this life.

And it is good that they start learning at an early age, so by the time they become older they will know how to deal and stand strong in the midst of the trials and temptations that we all must go through.

(Lam. 3:28) He sits alone, keeping quiet, because he has tolerated it on himself.

He remains quiet in isolation, being still, it is because God has brought it out of him because he had contact with him, God subjected him to suffering, and his particular way of talking in the earth so he might have the opportunity to be able to believe, and trust in God.

This person was sitting all by himself, and while he is doing this, he is very quiet, because God made this come out of him, it came out when God spoke to him, this was the contact he made with the man, God also exposed him to pain, and suffering.

He sits by himself, remaining quiet because this person was putting up with what was coming out of him, and putting up with the pain and suffering that God had exposed him to.

When it says, God subjected him to his particular way of talking in the earth, God would talk to the prophets, and then the prophets that lived on the earth would speak for him, this was his particular way of talking on the earth.

God would do this so, man would have the opportunity to know that God was real, and be able to believe in him, and come to trust him. And without prophets God would not have been able to speak to man, and man would not have been able to hear from God.

And when God spoke to a prophet you could say that when he spoke his words they went inside of the prophet's body, and his body was made of earth, so when God spoke this was also his particular way of speaking into the earth that was inside of a man.

(Lam. 3:29) He puts his mouth into the dust, if in this there might be some trust.

God put's his mouth into the dust; he uses this as a way to make the man become humble, and through this God is trying to find some hope in him, this is how the Lord brings hope out of the man.

When it says, he puts his mouth into the earth, God allows pain, and sorrow to humble the man so much that it causes him to fall on his knees, and when he falls his face falls to the ground which puts his mouth into the earth.

And when he falls and cries out to God his cries show God, he has hope, he is showing God he has hope because he is crying out to God.

(Lam. 3:30) He gives his cheek to him who hits him: he is fully filled up with disgrace.

He surrenders his cheek to the one who would hit him, God allows it to be struck hard so he will give up control: God wants him to give up total control, because he is totally filled up with a difficult way of thinking, and he is disgraced, and discredited because of the sin that is in his body.

He relinquishes control by yielding to the pain that is inflicted on him when his cheek is slapped, God allowed it to be hit, because he needed to experience suffering, so the man will stop trying to control his life.

And his thoughts do not line up with what God wants him to think, his thoughts are problematic, and that is why he needs to allow God to take control: and the things this man has suffered have caused him to be completely humiliated and have disgraced him.

(Lam. 3:31) Because the Lord will not throw away forever.

Because he does not want to throw anyone away forever:

God allowed this to happen to this man because he wanted to save him and not have to get rid of him forever, that was not what he wanted to do.

(Lam. 3:32) However though he causes mental suffering, still will he have kindness in agreement to the great number of his blessings.

Despite the fact that he brings about suffering in the mind, he still wishes to have a deep kindness that keeps with the great number of his many gifts and benefits.

(Lam. 3:33) Because he does not willingly trouble the children of men.

But he does not voluntarily cause any grief to the children of men.

(Matt. 5:39) But I say to you, that you are not to oppose. evil: but whoever will strike you on the right cheek, turn your other cheek to them and let them strike it too.

But I tell you, you are not to fight against evil: and whoever hits your right cheek, turn, and let them hit the other cheek too.

(Lk. 6:29) And to him who hits you on the one cheek offer him the other as well; and he who takes away your cloak do not stop them from taking your coat as well.

To the person who slaps you on one cheek present the other to him too: whoever takes your cape don't stop them and give them your coat too.

These verses are saying, if someone slaps your right cheek turn, and let them slap the left cheek too. He does afflict us, but it is something he really does not want to do, nor does he enjoy giving us grief, but he does it because of the grief that we give him, and the grief that we bring to our own lives.

His grief teaches us life's lessons; the grief we produce destroys our quality of life; the grief God produces improves our quality of life. If someone comes along, and takes your cape, do not fight to get it back, and do not cry over it, turn to them, and give them your coat as well.

Why? Because if they took your cape (cloak) that means they needed it, and if they needed it, give them your coat too, because they probably needed that too. We know that God will always take care of us, and he will provide you with another cape, and coat because he takes care of all our needs.

(Col. 1:9) For this reason we as well, since the day we heard it, do not stop praying for you, and crave that you might be filled up with the awareness of his will in all judgment, and spiritual intelligence.

The meaning of this verse is, since Paul and Timothy got the news of the saints in Colosse Paul wrote the letter of Colossians to them, letting them know he and Timothy were praying to God on their behalf.

And for them to want things from God, and to request

to be made whole in the truths of God, this was his desire for them to be made whole, in knowledge, and in all spiritual intelligence.

(Col. 1:10) That you may walk being worthy of the Lord in the directions of all that is pleasing, abounding in all good actions, and growing great in the intelligence of God.

We are to walk in our lives being important to the Lord, moving in our lives in the actions of all that is pleasing to God, being filled up on the inside in all the good deeds that the spirit has put in us. Constantly having life, becoming greater in the truths, facts, and principles of God.

Paul was praying that they would be pleasing to the Lord, and was praying to the Lord on their behalf, that through the prayers he, and Timothy sent up before the Lord, the Lord would grant the Colossians his Holy Spirit.

And this Holy Spirit would satisfy their inner man, and would make them whole in front of God, and this would please God even more. He was advising them to pray for the same things they were praying for which would please God too.

Paul was trying to teach them what to do to please the Lord, and how to do it, what manner to pray in, and what to pray for, and he was telling them what they would get should their prayers be pleasing to God.

He told them they would get what they were asking for, to be made whole, in the truths of God, and this would happen because of them getting the recognized knowledge, and kingdom mindset of God.

This knowledge that they have been told to ask for would make it possible for them to have the character they needed to be a delight, and it would please the Lord.

And it is the character of the Holy Spirit that makes us valuable to God, and we have to do what pleases him until we have fully made him happy.

And when we have made him happy, we grow greatly in the full righteousness of God, and we do this through the works we do for him, and in all we go through for him. All these things that we do for him, to please him, helps us to grow stronger in the Lord's truth's .

Divine Favor

To be divine means you come from God; divine also means having a God like character that can only be given by God.

When we belong to God this means we are favored by him, and this is a kindness that God shows to all his children, this is what God uses to befriend us; by doing this he is showing partiality to us too.

The word partiality means that he has a fondness for us, and he really likes us. All the scriptures that are below fall under divine favor, these scriptures tell us how God feels about us when we please Him, he is like a proud father who rewards his obedient children with grace, and mercy.

(Gen. 4:4) And Abel, had brought the first of his flock and the plumpest of them. And the Lord respected Abel and his gift:

Abel brought the first born of his animals, he brought the animals who were the freshest and the most well-fed of all of them, he brought the best of his flock to give to the Lord. And the Lord honored Abel, and his gift:

Because of the gift Abel gave to the Lord, Abel received God's divine favor.

(Gen. 6:8) But Noah found divine favor in the eyes of the LORD.

But Noah found divine favor in the LORD's eyes.

(Gen. 39:21) The Lord went with Joseph, and he was

able to see his divine favor and he gave him divine favor with the people who were guarding the prison.

The Lord was with Joseph, and because he was with Joseph, Joseph was able to see the Lord's divine favor working in his life. Then God gave him divine favor with those who guarded the jail.

(Ex. 2:25) God looked on the children of Israel and God had divine favor towards them.

God glanced down on the children of Israel and had divine favor for them.

(Ex. 33:12) And Moses said to the LORD, Look, you say to me, you want me to bring this people up out of Egypt: and you have not let me know who you will send with me. But you have said, I know you by your name, and you have as well-found favor in my eyes.

Moses said to the LORD, I noticed that you are saying to me, that you want me to bring this people out of Egypt: and you haven't told me who you are planning to send with me. But you have told me, I know you, and I know your name, and you have found favor in my sight.

(1 Sam. 2:26) And the child Samuel grew onward and had favor with both the LORD and men.

Samuel was a child when he was given the LORD's favor, and as he grew up, he was given the favor of both the LORD and men.

(2 Kings 13:23) And the LORD was pleasantly kind to them, and had love above them, and had respect for them, due to his covenant with Abraham, Isaac, and Jacob, and would not kill them, nor throw them out from his presence thus far.

And the LORD was pleasant, and loving to them, and he had love in the heaven's above them, and he had honor for them, because of the agreement that he made with Abraham, Isaac, and Jacob, and he would not kill them, or throw them away from his presence, so far anyway.

(Prov. 8:35) Because whoever finds me finds life and will gain favor of the LORD.

Anyone who seeks him out, and finds him, they will also find eternal life, and they will be given the favor of the LORD.

(Prov. 12:2) A good man obtains favor of the LORD: but a man of evil intentions will be punished.

A good man gains the favor of the LORD: but a man who is of wickedness, his actions will be penalized.

(Lk. 1:30) And the angel said to her, fear not, Mary: because you have found favor with God.

Then the angel spoke to her, do not fear, Mary: because you have built a firm belief in God, and you now have favor with him.

(Acts 7:46) Who found favor in front of God and yearned to find a place of worship for the God of Jacob.

It was David in this verse who found favor in the presence of God, and it was David who wanted to find a place of worship for the God of Jacob.

God's divine favor will open doors when you think none can be opened, and I know this to be true because I have seen him do it over and over again. His divine favor can lay a blessing in your lap when you are to the point in your life that you believe God has forgotten all about you.

He never forgets us, he may be delayed in answering our prayers, but he never forgets us. He allows things to go on in our lives for a time because he uses those situations to mold us and make us inside, now he can't remove them right away or they will not do the work he wants done inside of us.

The word says that he is the potter, and we are the clay, that means he as the potter takes us into his hands, and molds us like clay, molding our lives into whatever shape he wants them to be.

It is not up to us to mold ourselves; we have to trust in the God of our salvation to know what is best for us to be made into.

When making us he has to be patient, this he has to be, because it can take years in our time for him to develop us into the people that he wants us to be, praise the Lord.

I am living under his divine favor, and I love the fact that he loved me way back when he hung on the cross for me before I was even born, and that he loves me now that I have an earthly life.

And it is because of his divine favor, and his grace and mercy towards us that we have to put all our faith in him while allowing him to fight the battles for us.

Because we belong to him, we have to trust him, and believe that those who stand in opposition to us stand in opposition to him, and he will not take that lightly.

He does not like anyone doing harm to his children, but when what they have done works his perfect will, he will deal swiftly with the one who offended us, and just as one can be unfairly convicted God is able to send someone into their life when he is ready to give back to them what they deserve for the wrongs that they have done to his children.

We must continue to be patient, talking to him at all times, seeking his face day and night, and remembering that he is sitting on his throne looking down into our lives, and looking over our situations, always having the answers to the things we deem impossible to deal with, nothing is impossible for God, our lives are in his hands.

All things are possible to those of us who truly believe in him, he is our strength and our joy. He has given my life joy not just because he is in my life, but because he is God.

THE COMFORT OF GOD

God comforts us, he soothes us, he consoles us, he reassures us, he makes us physically comfortable, he gives us support, he encourages us, and he is our relief in hard times.

(2 Cor. 1:3) Worthy of adoration is God, indeed the Father of our Lord Jesus Christ, the Father of forgiveness, and the God of comfort.

Praise be to the God who is truly the Father of our Lord Jesus Christ, the Father of mercy, and the God of all comfort.

(2 Cor. 1:4) Who comforts us in every one of our troubles, that we might be prepared to bring comfort to those who are in any kind of trouble, with the comfort by which we are comforted ourselves by God.

Who comforts us in all our troubles, so that we can comfort those who are in trouble with the comfort we ourselves have received from God.

(2 Cor. 1:5) Because the pains of Christ overflows to us, so our comfort also overflows through Christ.

Because just as the sufferings of Christ flows over into us, so in the same way through Christ does our comfort overflow.

Jesus sufferings flood out of him into us, and his comfort floods out of him into us too. The pains that Jesus suffered flows out of him into us, and so as well does our comfort flow out of us through Christ Jesus.

The comfort that floods out of him into us is the Holy Spirit, and the Holy Spirit also is his sufferings that flood into us as well.

(2 Cor. 1:6) And if we are troubled, it is for your comfort and deliverance, that is the result of the tolerance of the same distresses that we also suffer: or whether we are soothed, it is because of your comfort and deliverance.

If we are distressed, it is for your comfort, and deliverance; and if we are comforted, it is for the comfort, that is produce in you, it is produced through your patient endurance of the same sufferings that we suffer.

If we are in pain, it is so you will be comforted, and also you will be able to be saved, the outcome of this is that you will be able to endure the same afflictions that we as well have suffered: if we are comforted it is done for your comfort, and freedom.

The hardships that the disciples, and Paul went through, they had to go through them so those in the future would have the right to be comforted by the same Holy Spirit that came back, and comforted the disciples, and Paul.

They suffered so we would see their example in the future and have faith that if they could endure the sufferings that they did in the past so those of us in the future would be able to have the right to salvation, then we could endure sufferings for our future generations.

I now understand that what they did, they did to spiritually set us free, just as Jesus made it possible for all men to be set free, they followed in his footsteps.

(2 Cor. 1:7) And our hope for you is firm in purpose, knowing that you are participants of the sufferings, so you will also be of the comforted.

And our hope for you is firm because we know that just as you share in our sufferings, so also you share in our comfort.

And our concern for you is strong in its intent, realizing that you are partaker's of the sufferings, and so you as well will be of the many children who will be comforted.

Show admiration to the Father of our Lord Jesus Christ, who is a Father of deep sympathy, and a God of all reassurance. He consoles us in all our afflictions, and troubles. And because he reassures us his reassurance makes it possible for us to support others with the encouragement God has placed in us.

If we distress it is so God will come and comfort you and continue to bring salvation into your life. God has many ways to console us, we just have no idea of the ways he is able to console us.

In ones being consoled by God it produces spiritual calmness along with lasting spiritual strength that comes by the same pains we all have to withstand. We all share in each other's pains, and we all share in each other's support.

(Matt. 5:4) Blessed are those who grieve: because they will be comforted.

Those who are feeling great sorrow are blessed: and because they are blessed, they will be comforted.

(Matt. 9:20) And look, a woman, who had a disease that was of her blood that was flowing out of her for 12 yrs., she came up behind him, and grabbed the hem of his garment:

There was a women who had a problem with her monthly blood flow for 12 yrs., who walked up behind Jesus, and latched onto the hem of his clothing:

(Matt. 9:21) Because she said inside of herself, suppose I, if I grab his garment, I will be healed.

The reason she did what she did was that she spoke to

herself on the inside and said, I believe that if I grab his clothing, I will become healthy.

(Matt. 9:22) But Jesus turned himself around, and when he saw her, he said, Daughter, be of good comfort; your faith has made you whole. And the woman was made whole from that hour.

But Jesus turned around, and when he laid his eyes on her he said, daughter, you be of good comfort; your faith has healed you. and the woman was made spiritually right from that specific moment.

Jesus told this woman; daughter be of good comfort; your faith has made you whole. The comfort Jesus gave her was good comfort, good in this verse means of the highest quality, that was righteous, and excellent.

Only the highest quality of comfort would be found in Jesus, he would not have any other kind; his comfort came directly from the throne of the Father in heaven.

He soothed the problem of her blood that she had for 12 years, because of the faith she activated when she chose to believe in him, he consoled the pain of the sickness she carried.

He reassured her that when she touched the hem of his garment she pulled the love out of him, and she gave him something in return, her faith. And in giving her faith to him she became whole she was healed.

The word whole means what had gone wrong in her body was repaired by Jesus making her healthy, because of her faith, she was no longer sick, she was no longer broken, she was no longer in pain, this woman's faith made Jesus very happy.

When he called her daughter, he was referring to her as his child, and letting her know that he was her father, and he was a father who was comforting his child, who had been sick, and then he healed his daughter of her disease.

And he did not get angry at her because she pulled on him, he did not keep his love from her, she drew it out, and he welcomed what she did, and welcomed her with open arms into his kingdom, she made him very happy.

One more thing we as the children of God are supposed to pull on him, this is what he wants us to do, pull and be persistent in what we are pulling on him for, in what we want from him.

(Jn. 14:18) I am not going to leave you without any comfort: I will come back to you.

Jesus is letting his children know that he would make sure they were comforted after his death, and that he would come back to them after his death on the cross in the form of the comforter.

(Jn. 14:26) But the one who will comfort, that is the Holy Ghost, who the Father is going to send in my name, he will instruct you in all the things of God and will bring all of Gods things back to your memory, everything that I have said to you.

The one that will comfort you is the Holy Ghost, who the Father will send in my name, he will teach you all things, and bring it back to your memory, whatever I have said to you.

So, the comforter is the Holy Ghost, this is his assignment to be the comforter, so he can comfort the children of God. While Jesus walked in the earth with the spirit inside of him, the Holy Spirit was a spirit but once he died, and once the spirit was no longer inside his earthly body it became the Holy Ghost, death must come in order for a spirit to become a ghost.

The comforter was sent back to God's children in the power, and authority of Jesus Christ. He came to do the work of the Father in the earth in his children. It teaches us all about all the things of God and makes us remember whatever Jesus says to us. It ushers us into the Holy places of God in his tabernacle, and reveals the deep secrets of his belongings, the Holy Ghost knows all things yes, the deep things that belong to God.

(Rom. 15:4) Seeing that whatever events were written previously were written in the interest of your education, so we through patience, and comfort of the scriptures may have faith.

In view of the fact that no matter what important happenings were written of earlier, it was written because it concerned your spiritual development, you needed to be taught spiritual knowledge, like how to spiritually reason, and how to judge according to the spirit. In order that we through patience, and the comfort of the scriptures can believe in Christ Jesus.

(1 Cor. 14:3) But he who foretells of things to come (prophesies) speaks to men to uplift (edification) them, and to advise (exhortation) them, and to comfort them.

Still the one who talks about things that are to come, he is talking to men to help them to spiritually improve, and to council them, and to reassure (comfort) them.

When one prophesies, they are doing it to help the person they are talking to, because they are trying to help them spiritually grow, so they will be able to spiritually advance.

The more they grow, the more spiritual they become, and the more spiritual they become the more they leave the flesh behind. They also talk to them because they know they need to be counseled, so basically, they need a counselor, because they need someone to advise them in holy matters.

And lastly, they talk to them to help relieve the pains that they may be going through as they suffer for Christ's sake.

It's hard when hard times hit someone, sometimes it seems

as though you are getting hit back-to-back, and you just pray for a little relief.

Then someone shows up, and gives you comforting words, this could only happen because God sent them with the comforter on the inside of them, to give the kind of comfort every soul needs during the hard times that are necessary for us to go through in the name of Jesus.

(Eph. 6:22) Who I have sent to you for the same reason, so you may know our business, and he may comfort your hearts.

This person I sent to you for this reason, so you will know the work that we do, and so he can reassure (comfort) your hearts.

This person was sent to do all of the above, but also to let these people know about the duties that they were performing for Christ sake, they wanted them to know all about God's business.

(2 Cor. 1:14) Since you as well have admitted that we are real to some extent, in that we are your delight, still you as well are ours in the light of the Lord Jesus.

Because you in addition have confirmed that we are genuine somewhat, in that we happen to be your joy, even so you too are ours in the brightness of Jesus Christ.

Because these people have accepted that the writer of this scripture, and all the other's with him were for real in the testimonies about the Lord, and that they did live.

But they were only able to prove it to a point, but even still knowing about them made these people very happy, so happy they were filled with joy, and knowing about these people made the writer, and his people very happy too, they saw them as illuminating lights that were a part of the Lord Jesus Christ.

THE HEALING OF GOD

(2 Chr. 7:14) If my people, who are called by my name, will humble themselves, pray, and search for my face, and move away from there evil ways, then I will hear from heaven, and I will pardon their sin, and I will cure their land.

If the people who are called by my name, would kneel before me, and pray to me, and search out my face, and change and then move away from their wicked ways, I will hear my people while I am sitting in heaven.

And I will forgive their sins, and I will make everything in them right, and I will heal their condition. The condition he is talking about healing in them is ground (land), that is their bodies that have a certain condition in them, the sinful condition that every man has to live with.

(Mal. 4:2) But to you who fear my name will the Sun of righteousness appear with healing in his wings; and you will go forward and grow up like young who are taken care of by the Lord.

To you who are in awe of me, and my name, you who look forward to the glory of Jesus to show up with the cure for sin, he will come to make all his people spiritually whole, through the power that comes with him.

His people who are under his protection will move forward, so they can mentally, and physically mature, and come to be spiritually lifted up, then their spiritual situation will be made better. Like the young who are brought to a standstill, and who are ready to be fed under the protection of the Lord.

And all of this the Lord does for those who honor him, and are in awe of him, this is one of the stipulation for being healed, if you do not honor him, you will not receive all that he has for those who do as he instructs.

The Sun of righteousness, the shinning source of the proper glory of God is Jesus Christ. He is the Son of God, he is the Sun of glory, the Son of Light, the source of knowledge, he is all, and is in all.

He is the one who possesses the cure, and he is the conclusion to all sin. He is the one who is able to make all spiritually healthy, and sound. To be sound is to be healthy, and to be free of damage or injury, defect, or disease.

This is what Jesus is able to do, he is able to reunite us with the Father, and when he reunites us, we are no longer spiritually broken, and no longer separated from God.

We are reunited once again with him, and this makes us spiritually healthy, putting us in good standing with God, putting us in a good condition mentally, and spiritually. Our reunion gives us a spiritually solid character, and this is a quality that pleases God.

The word sound also means that when we are obedient and give our lives to Jesus then we are given a noise that comes from our spirits that God is able to hear from us because we are no longer sinners.

Before being made whole the flesh had a voice, but when we are made whole the voice of the flesh begins to die, and the voice of the Holy Spirit begins to resonate with a sound that only comes from the heavens.

When the Holy Ghost is given to us, we receive a certain tone in our voices that has a certain musical quality to it that sounds wonderful in the ears of the Lord, in the realm of the spirit. This tone sings praises to God in a way that the noise that came from us in sin could never do, it was earthly, and sinful, and God's ears does not hear the sound of a sinful man because it does not come from the Holy Spirit, it comes from his flesh, and the word says "God does not listen to the sinful man, but he watches over, and gives his ear to his elect.

(Acts 10:38) By what means did God anoint Jesus of Nazareth with the Holy Ghost and having power: who did go about doing good and curing everyone who was burdened by Satan, because God was with him.

For this reason, God put his holy oil of the Holy Spirit on Jesus of Nazareth, that came with great power, and it had the authority of his Father, and because of his character, and his position of importance as the son of God he went forward in his unity with his Father.

Carrying out his Father's righteous works, doing his spiritual healing, and his purification, and freeing his people from sin. Who were under the control of Lucifer because they were being ruled by him, and were bound to his troublesome, cruel ways.

Because he had been anointed with the ointment of the Holy Ghost Jesus had great strength, and was very mighty in the heavens, and he had the authority of his Father to do everything that he did as he walked on the earth. His character was that of his Father, holy, and his position of importance was being the only son of God.

And because of all he was he was equipped to perform

and do the works of the spiritual will of his Father by making people spiritually healthy, and helping them to grow spiritually, purifying them, and releasing them from the grip Lucifer had on them.

All power, and authority was given to Jesus Christ, and because it was, he was able to stop Lucifer from suppressing the souls of his children, and stopped him from making them spiritually sick, and he stopped him from putting them down, and weighing them down in sin.

Jesus was able to subdue him because he came with the power of the Father in him, and his Father was with him to help him get the work done.

Jesus stayed connected with the Father, being in an intimate relationship with his Father, and he did everything he saw his Father do, everything he heard his Father say, and he followed his Father's instructions, Jesus was a faithful son; the kind of Son God wants us to be.

THE LOVE OF GOD 1

God's love for you has no conditions; and it never ends, that is the reason God gave us love because when we have nothing else to give, we are always able to give love. Love is plentiful, it lasts forever, even after we leave this earthly realm.

It does not matter where we go in life or who we leave behind we will always have love. Love is not conditioned on who we are to the people in our lives; there is no price for us to pay for love, because Jesus paid the price for loving us on calvary.

(Jn. 3:16) Due to the fact that God really loved this world, that he gave his only Son, so anyone who believes in him will not die, but they will have eternal life.

God loved us so much, that he gave his only son, because he wanted to give the world the right to believe in his son, and once they did, they would be given eternal life.

(Jn. 3:17) Because God did not send his Son into the world to judge the world; just that the world through him might be saved.

God did not send his son into the world to condemn the world, he wanted the world to be saved through his son.

(Jn. 3:18) He who believes on him will not be found guilty: but he who believes not is already found guilty, because he has not believed in the name of the only child who is the

Son of God.

Those who dared to believe on him would not be judged: at that time the ones who don't believe are already convicted, because it is their disbelief in Jesus Christ that convicts them, and this is because they have chosen not to believe in the name of the only son of God.

Jesus sacrifice was proof enough of how much God loved us, he loved us so much, and his love for us was so strong that he allowed himself to be killed.

I say allowed because he was God in the flesh, and at any time he could have stopped his death, but he did not because his Father's purpose was greater, and he came down to earth to do just what he knew had to be done, he had to do what pleased his Father.

He allowed mankind to kill him so he could shed his blood for us, because he, and his Father knew that his blood, his life was what we needed to cleanse us from all unrighteousness and save us from the snares of Satan.

Love does not stop just because one is out of eye site, or away for a long period of time, love is something God is able to plant in all of us, and when he does it only grows because God makes it grow. It has no end, and when we allow God to help us to tap into it, it is the most beautiful thing that God has ever blessed us with.

Hope in it, live in it, breath it in, and never give up on it, always nurture it, and it will nurture you. The word nurture means to feed, and protect, and it also means to support and encourage like during a period of training, and development we are to care for it and cherish it.

So, if we feed, protect, support, and encourage love, if

we take care of it, and cherish it, and know the reason for this is because love is Jesus Christ himself then God will do all of the above in the scripture's for us our whole entire lives, and during these periods of our lives, he is developing our characters, the characters of the true children of God, and training our spirits in spiritual matters, and spiritual warfare.

He uses his love for us to make us, and it is an intricate part of our development, it is very necessary for us to get to where he intends for us to go in his spiritual affairs. If one does not have love, and if they do not have God, all they do is done for nothing.

(Eph. 5:25) Husbands, love your wives, still as Christ as well loved the church, and gave himself for it.

Husbands are to love their wives, just as Jesus Christ also loved the church, and sacrificed himself for it.

(Eph. 5:28) In this way men ought to love their wives like they love their own bodies. He who loves his wife loves himself.

In this fashion men are to love their wives in the same way they love their own bodies. The man who loves his wife should love her like he loves himself.

(Eph. 5:33) However, let each one of you in this instance love his wife as they love themselves; and the wife should make sure that she deeply honors her husband.

Nevertheless, allow each one of you in this example to love his wife like they love themselves; and the wife is to make sure that deep down inside she respects her husband.

Love is the main foundation that Jesus' teachings are built on, his word says love is the greatest thing a man and woman could ever have in their hearts for each other when they are husband and wife.

(1 Cor. 13:1) Although I talk with the tongue of men and of angels, and do not have love, I have become like a sounding brass, or like a tinkling cymbal.

Though I speak with the tongue of men, and angels, and do not have love, I have come to be like the sound of brass, or like a jingling cymbal.

Without love we are spiritually dead, and when a person verbally expresses themselves all they have is the fleshly sound of their earthly voice, no godly life is heard in them because there is no Holy Spirit in them.

They are just as fleshly as they were before they claimed to know him, when there is no Holy Spirit there is no love. This is what it means when this verse says he has become like a sounding brass, or like a tinkling cymbal.

Though this person speaks with the language (tongue) of a man using the spiritual words of the angels, there still will be no life in a sound like this.

Brass is the metal that is symbolic of the earthly man, and his fleshly nature, and the tinkling symbols are made of brass. When they are struck all, you can hear are vibrations, and basically that is what is heard when one speaks without the Holy Spirit.

A vibrating sound, but no spiritual life will be heard in them, and the love of Jesus will not be seen in them either, no Godly love is experienced from them, and there is no Spirit filled music from the Holy Spirit in them either.

(1 Pet. 1:22) Considering that you have made your souls

clean by following the truth through the Holy Spirit to the pure love of the brothers, and make sure you love one another with a real heart that has a wonderful strength to it.

Considering that you did accept freedom from sin, and your souls did follow who is real, and faithful, then you did complete the process through the Holy Ghost to the sincere, and genuine love of the brothers.

You need to understand that you are to love each other as you have loved the first, the first one being Jesus Christ. Having an undefiled heart, and loving intensely with passion, and a burning only the Holy Ghost can supply you with.

Love is something that can't be destroyed or extinguished; it is not corruptible or changeable. It means you no harm and can do no harm; there is no hatred in it, no malice, no envy, and no jealousy, only pure love, only Gods love.

Love can be shown, and it can be acted on, in a look, or a touch, or a thought, or in being still or being able to place all things in the life of those you care about in the hands of God.

There are many ways to show love for someone or for one another, love is not something you have to demand from someone, love is something that is freely given from the heart, and whatever is given from the heart is a gift from God.

THE LOVE OF GOD 2

(Rom. 12:9) Let love be without attitude. Detest what is wicked; stick closely to what is good.

Let love be without deception, it must be for real, and true from the heart, dislike what is not of the nature of God, that is evil, and hold tight to what is holy, good, and righteous.

(Rom. 12:10) Be kind in your heart in the affections that you have for one another and do this in brotherly love; you are to do this while honoring your brother; and while making sure that you prioritize each other in this love.

Continue in unity, being pleasant, and gentle, having a fond connection for each other, and be loving to one another, and have a friendship for each member, that is of a nature that is of a different period of time, that has been spoken of as being loving, with a love that will be befitting of a brother, being very loyal, and having a deep tenderness, and loving affection for one another.

That is in a fashion of great respect, and you will be given this favor in return, we are to show a love that is very distinctive in how love was once shown. What is meant when I say it is of a different period of time, I mean this kind of love was shown in the distant past, in a time long forgotten, when the people of God were truly united.

(Rom. 12:11) Be not lazy in business; burning in spirit; serving the Lord.

Do not be lazy or idle in the office of the calling God has

given you, always feeling enthusiasm in serving him, always being on spiritual fire for him, and always showing the Lord you are in his service.

(Rom. 12:12) Be joyful in your belief; be calm in tribulations, be persistent and demanding as you move on in prayer.

Always expressing joy, and expressing it often, always celebrating he who is the reason for the expectations we have, him being the expectation itself.

We carry the expectation that belongs to him, that is his hope, quietly, and steadily being persistent, being diligent in his sufferings, pains, distresses, and grief.

We have to keep on going, pressing with an urgency, in how we spiritually talk to God, doing this in sincere prayers in front of Him. No matter what happens in the course of our lives in Christ Jesus, being ever faithful in our prayers to the almighty God.

(Rom. 12:13) Dealing out to the needs of the saint's, who have the tendency to be friendly.

Always giving what you have to help Gods people who are in need of what you give them, and always being cordial, and generous to others.

The word cordial means we are to be courteous, gracious, friendly, and warm. We are to be sincere, and our sincerity is to be real, and heartfelt, it is not supposed to be done from the feelings of the flesh, in the flesh we can't do this, only in the Spirit can it be done.

We are to present ourselves in the power of the Holy Ghost, and only by the Holy Ghost can we be cordial and stimulating. Only the Holy Ghost can stimulate, it is by stimulation of the Holy Ghost that God is able to resurrect those who are not able to show love or be generous to others.

(Rom. 12:14) Bestow good to those who cause you pain: give good to them and don't speak curses over them.

Ask God to give divine favor to anyone who pursues you by harassing you or by trying to oppress you, give good of any kind to them, and do not ask God to harm them.

God is a loving God, and all he wants to do for us is to bring us to him, and to place salvation on us. If he would do this for us while we were yet in our mess, how much more does he want to do for those who are still in theirs.

And their pursuing of us in wickedness is not a means for God to change the desire he has for them, but he will use their pursuit of us to bring them to his side if this is his will, he will use what he will use to get the work done.

And their pursuit of us God will use to get a righteous prayer sent up in front of his throne on the pursuers behave, so he can stop their pursuit of us, and their cause for pursuing us. We were created for God's use, whatever it takes to bring one to salvation, God's will, will be done on earth as it is in heaven.

(Rom. 12:15) Be glade with those who are glade, and cry with them who cry.

Take delight, and glorify God with those who are joyful, and cry with those who experience great sorrow. Make a joyful noise to the Lord, and glorify his name together, take pleasure in him, and know that he is God, please him greatly as one. Cry before him, express grief, shed your tears, but do it all together as one in front of him in his presence.

(Rom. 12:16) You are to have the same mind concerning each other. Don't be mindful of the things of the wealthy of this world, and do not stoop down to the behavior of men who are of poor heritage. Do not think that you are smart in your own ideas.

Always live with this kind of spiritual character because this character has the quality of intelligence, and understanding, and always have this personality with one another.

Refuse to take heed to matters that are the affairs of the extravagant, this is talking about luxuries that the rich indulge in.

And always be ready to behave as if you are aware of the fact that you could descend down into sin from your spiritually high position to assume the position that all mankind of the earth are in, they are in this position because they are living a brought down existence, due to the fact that they are still living in sin.

And refuse to do the deeds of trickery or craftiness, these are in one's personal control, and men are able to conceive of these sinful things in their own thoughts, and ideas.

(Rom. 12:17) Do not give in return to any man evil for evil. Only give those things that are true in the eyesight of every man.

Repay no man with evil even though they may have been evil to you. Make available to them important truths that are honorable, that are in your mind, using the knowledge that you have been given, and always have concern for every man.

We must not give back to a person the evil that they have chosen to give to us while walking in sin, we must give them the knowledge, wisdom, and the intellect of the Holy Ghost that lives inside of us. We must walk in the nature, and the integrity of the teachings of our Lord, and Savior Jesus Christ.

We must always be willing to teach what the reasons are for the hope that God has placed inside of us, and to show this person that there is another way, and another life that is so much better than the one they know and are accustomed to. We are illuminating lights in a dying world, and we are the here, and now symbol of the hope of our Lord Jesus Christ, people need to know.

(Rom. 12:18) If it is possible to achieve, with everything that is within you, try to live in peace with every man.

Hypothetically speaking, and as mentioned before you can live, to the fullest extent, because it is inside you, to continue to have life when we choose to have no strife or hostility with anyone.

Strife, and hostility can destroy a person from the inside out, and it causes a separation between God, and the one who has chosen to be angry.

When this separation takes place it causes a spiritual death, and in order to cause a reuniting of the person, with God the person who got angry has to do some serious repenting, and only when God is pleased with how they have repented then will he reunite with the person.

So, in order for this not to happen we must avoid anger, and strife with anyone, and in doing so God will be pleased. We do not want spiritual things that are not pleasing to God to rise up in us after we have been warned not to do it, these are the things that consist inside of us, we must take charge of them, and master them through the power of the Holy Ghost.

(Rom. 12:19) Those I love very much, do not try to take

revenge yourselves, just be willing to allow the anger to be done to you: because it is written, that revenge is mine; and I will return it back to them for you, said the Lord.

The Lord is saying that we don't have to try to take revenge on anyone who chooses to point their anger in our direction because he sees all, and he knows all, and he loves us so much that he wants us not to concern ourselves with the situation because he has already planned on handling it for us.

And his plan is to take revenge for us, and he plans to return to whoever is angry with us what they dished out to us, because this is his job. This falls under his taking care of his children, so we won't have a worry in this world, and so we can be at peace, in the way he wants us to be, because he is the one who loves us very much.

(Rom. 12:20) So, if your enemy feels hungry, feed him; if he needs a drink, give him a drink: the reason for this is in doing this you will be unloading charcoals of fire on his head.

For this reason, should the person who feels hatred towards you, need food, then supply him with nourishment, and minister to him, so you can satisfy his soul.

On the condition he is longing for knowledge, voluntarily give it to him, give him what is suitable for him to eat, the purpose of this is over a period of time in the way indicated to you.

You will be filling the person up with the abundant fuel that will make them be able to spiritually ignite, and this will spiritually unite them with the Lord of glory.

And then they will become one who will belong to him, and they will be put in their place to become one with the great authority, power, and honor of our Lord Jesus Christ.

(Rom. 12:21) Do not be taken by surprise by sin but overcome sin with good.

Refuse to allow immorality to get the victory over you, on the other hand, choose to win against the wickedness of the day by opposing it, and by walking, and living upright in Christ Jesus.

We are not to let sin, and wickedness take us over, we are not supposed to give into it, we are supposed to deny it access to us in our new life.

And we are supposed to fight it, and have in our minds that we are going to defeat it by living a much better, upright, and morally excellent life in Christ Jesus. Not giving into the standards of the society that we have to live in today, we are better than that because of Christ being in our lives. And if we were to live as everyone else who is not in Christ then what was the purpose for giving our lives to him? We might as well have stayed in the wretched condition we were in.

(Mk. 12:30) You will love the Lord your God with all your heart, and with all your soul, and with all your mind, and with every bit of your strength: this is the first commandment.

You will love the Lord your God completely with your heart, and completely with your soul, and completely with your mind, and completely with your moral power, you will obey him.

And this was so ordered before all other orders were given. We are to love him with everything that is in us, in the way that he wants us to love him. If he loves us there should be no problem loving him in the way that he has asked us to love him.

THE MIND OF WISDOM

A couple of weeks ago I asked God how was Adam able to name everything? And after asking that question a couple of weeks later I noticed that I would be told to do something or asked to do something, but when I went to do it, and pictured it in my mind, what I pictured in my mind was what I did, not what I was asked to do.

For example: at this time, I was working in a print shop, and someone asked me to get them a pack of lilac paper, as I walked over to get the paper, I saw in my mind lilac being green, so I picked up the green paper.

The person I got the paper for came down to get it, and she said to me you got me green, not lilac; lilac is purple. So, I told her in my mind I saw lilac as being green, and as I walked away, I started to laugh, and so did she.

And I did not feel stupid, and I did not feel I had made a mistake because I only did what God showed me in my mind. Then when I was driving home it came to me how Adam named everything, he did it by divine inspiration of God; God spoke to his mind and showed him the names.

(Gen. 2:7) And the LORD God molded man using the topsoil of the ground in the Garden of Eden, and then he exhaled into the nostrils of his nose, giving him a light current of air that sent the spirit of life into him, and the man changed, and became an actively living soul.

God made Adam from the fertile topsoil of the ground of the Garden of Eden and his body initially was created a spiritual body of flesh when it was made in the Garden of Eden. And so, after making him a spiritual body of flesh, he then breathed the spirit into him.

Because God is a Holy Spirit, and the only thing he could put inside of Adam's spiritual body was the Spirit of Life, and in doing this Adam woke up and began moving in the spiritual realm, because he became a living, moving spiritual being.

Adam was not an earthly fleshly being before the fall, then after the fall he and Eve had to learn how to do things that beings of the earth outside of the Garden would have to learn how to do, because they were no longer living in the Garden of Eden, because God put them out, because of what they did.

God made us opposite of how he made Adam and Eve, Adam and Eve were made in the spiritual Garden of Eden and were given spiritual bodies, becoming spiritually alive beings in the garden, and were sent out to live in the world after they ate the fruit of the wrong tree.

Their spiritual flesh changed, and became flesh that sin now had control of, and this is how they came to be fleshly beings of the earth.

We are born into this world already being fleshly beings of the world; then when we come to Christ, we have to learn how to live a spiritual life through the Holy Spirit that is given to us by Jesus Christ.

(Gen. 3:23) And Adam said, this is now bone of my bones, and flesh of my flesh; she shall be called woman, because she was taken out of man.

Adam said that Eve was at that moment part of him, he said she was bone of his bones, and that she was of his flesh:

and that he would give her the name Woman, and his reason for calling her this name was because she was made from him, she was taken out of him, like a child is formed and taken out of the womb of its mother, she was taken out of Adam like he was a womb and that was the reason she was called woman. To me the word woman sounds like a combination of womb and man, woman.

When God formed Adam, and Eve this was his wisdom in action, he used his knowledge and know how to perform this great feat, no one else would have been able to do what God did.

(Lk. 25:45) Then opened he their understanding, that they might understand the scriptures,

At that time Jesus exposed his disciples' minds after his death to the power of God so they would have the enlightened intelligence of God, so they would be able to grasp the ideas of the scriptures and be able to interpret them.

They were not able to understand him after he rose from the dead because their minds were still closed to the understanding of the scriptures.

But once he died, he was able to help them understand what had happened, and what was still going to happen, and what he had to do according to what was written of him in the scriptures.

I love when the Lord brings a word to my mind and has me search out the meaning of the word that he has given me, and I find the word has several different meanings. Then he has me study the word and believe it or not that is how I got a lot of the topics I have written about in this book.

Just hearing a word in my mind. I walked around for

years with a bible, and a dictionary looking up the meanings of words I came across in the bible that I did not know the meaning of, or I just did not understand the word.

I did not realize just how doing this would expand my thoughts, and my vocabulary, I never thought one day I would have sought out knowledge, and I thought the knowledge that I got was because of the experiences in my life, not realizing the knowledge I got came from having God in my life, studying his word, life, and the dictionary, and all of it was arranged by God.

I didn't know what I had gotten because I was not using it until the day God gave me the order to write and share it with a friend. Once I started writing to this friend then I began to see just what God had put in me.

God has us do things in our lives for years, and we do not see the benefits of what he is having us do until one day he says get up and apply what I have shared with you.

When he calls some of us, we may think we can't do this all-important job he has placed in front of us, but he pushes us, and says yes you can do it, and you will do it.

We may not know what we are capable of, but God knows, so we take those steps to do what he wants us to do, and we are successful, because he is with us.

(1 K. 3:7) And at this time, O LORD my God, you have made your servant king in place of David my father: and I am just a little child: I do not know how to go out or come in.

And at this moment O LORD my God, you have made your servant king in place of my father David: but I am just a small child: I do not know how to leave a room or enter into one.

(1 K. 3:9) Grant in this your servant a heart that is able to comprehend and judge your people, so I may be able to recognize good and evil when I am in the middle of them: because who is able to judge your important people?

Give your servant in this matter a heart that can embrace, and judge your people, then I might be able to identify good, and evil at the time I am in the midst of them: the reason for this is who is able to govern such a large number of your very important people?

Solomon prayed this prayer for himself to be able to see good, and evil when he was around it, he wanted to be able to see the difference between the two.

And he knew he needed the Lord's help to be able to govern such a large number of his people, he knew he had to have a clear mind to be able to have the mental insight to govern his people, and he knew he could not do it by himself, as young as he was.

(1 K. 3:10) And the spoken words pleased the Lord, that Solomon had asked this thing.

Solomon talked to the Lord, and the words he spoke pleased him, and what he asked for also pleased him.

(1 K. 3:11) God said to Solomon, because you have asked for this, and have not ask for long life for yourself; nor have you asked for wealth for yourself, nor have you asked for your enemies to be destroyed; but you have asked me to make it possible for you to grasp ideas and to be able to figure out how to make choices.

God said to Solomon, due to the fact that you asked for this, and did not ask for yourself to be able to live a long life; neither did you ask for riches for yourself, neither did you ask that your enemies be killed.

But you asked me to arrange it for you to be able to pick up on ideas, and for you to be able to find out how to make decisions.

His request made God happy, because it was not a selfish request, he asked God to help him do right, and to be able to understand what is right.

(1 K. 3:12) Look, I have done according to your words: look, I have given to you an enlightened and understanding heart; in order that there would be none like you in front of you, nor after you will there be any to rise up like you.

See, I have complied with your words: See, I have given you a heart that is wise, and can understand; so there will not be anyone like you before you, and after you there will not be anyone who will show up who will be anything like you.

(1 K. 3:13) And I also have given you what you have not asked for, both wealth, and honor; in order that there will not be any in the midst of the kings like you all your days.

And I as well have given you what you have not asked me for, I gave you wealth and high respect; so there will not be anyone amongst the royals who will be like you all your days.

(1 K. 3:14) And if you will walk in my ways, and keep my statues, and my commands, like your father David did walk, then I will increase your days.

And if you will walk in my ways, and keep my set up, and my commands, like your father David walked, then I will extend your days.

Solomon's request pleased God, because Solomon's request was not selfish, because his request pleased God, God made Solomon wise, and gave him an understanding mind, and made it clear to Solomon that he had created him to be a one-of-a-kind king, he was a firstling, the first of his kind in the type of king that he was.

The mind Solomon had, no other man before him ever had, and no other man after him would have it either, except Jesus Christ, he was the only one to have the kind of wisdom Solomon had before him, and then some, because Jesus Christ was greater than Solomon.

Jesus wasn't a man who was created in sin, he was the Son of man, and he was a God, that is why he was able to be greater than Solomon, and that is why he had more wisdom than Solomon ever had.

Then God gave him what he had not asked for, both riches, and respect, so no other king would ever compare to Solomon, no other earthly king. Then he promised Solomon if he continued in his ways, keeping what he had set up, and doing his commandments like David his father had, then he would also make it so Solomon would live a long life.

God made Solomon a king, and it was not the wealth on earth that he received that made him royalty or honorable, it was because he accepted the Lord God almighty. And God did not give Solomon riches, and honor before he made sure he was wise, he gave these things to him after he knew he had made him wise.

Wisdom is a gift from God, foolishness is of man, and folly will not remain in those who are the chosen of God, folly can't, and will not exist before the Lord in the lives of his people.

Solomon thought of himself as being a child when he was placed on the throne of David his father. What made

Solomon no longer a boy, was his acceptance of Gods will, and his spoken favor to the Lord that he was God of his life! Solomon knew he could not be the king, and the man he needed to be to rule over his people without the knowledge, and wisdom of the God of his father.

He was raised by his father, and taught the commandments, and the laws of his father David's God. He was trained in the ways of the Lord, and he knew God was supposed to come first in whatever he did, and what he needed to do as king.

Solomon was also the 3rd king placed on the throne to rule over Israel at the time he became king, he was the king with the mind, and wisdom of God.

GOD SEES THE HEART, LOVE

Your heart is the center of you, and the essence of who you are, and it's where your life is. Sometimes the love in a person's heart is never shared because of the pains and hurts one may have experienced in their life.

And because of the pains and hurts one has had to suffer they shut down that loving side of themselves, and they only make available the hurtful parts of themselves because this is all life has taught them.

Really the only one you can truly give your heart to so it can be repaired is God, he is the only one we can really give anything spiritually to.

So, he can spiritually change us, and we can become his children, and our hearts are the part of us that God wants the most.

(1 Cor. 15:50) At this time I say this to you, brothers, flesh, and blood will not be the heirs of the kingdom of God; nor will corruption be an heir to incorruption.

Now I say to you, brothers, flesh, and blood will not be the ones who inherits God's kingdom; and sin will not be an inheritor of holiness either.

Anyone who follows after what their body craves and does not follow after the knowledge of the spirit, they won't inherit God's kingdom, his kingdom is not for those who are not living by the Holy Spirit; it is for the true children of God. And sin can't inherit what is holy, so if one is morally lacking there's no way that they will ever be given the right to receive as an heir, the kingdom of God.

(1 Pet. 3:4) Just allow it to be the secret man of the heart, in what is not able to be corrupted, but let it be the beautiful appearance of a gentle and peaceful Spirit, that is in the eyes of God of great price.

Just let it be the hidden man of the heart, that is not able to be made to become wicked, but let it be the beauty that is of the Holy Spirit that appears to have a gentleness, and peacefulness, and this beauty, and peace in God's eyes is of great value.

He wants the man that society probably will never see or except, God knows we can walk through this life only allowing a certain side of us to be seen.

He came to uncover the other side of us that this life can beat down so bad that we learn how to walk through it covering it up, this is the best part of us, and that is the part God wants from us the most.

That person lives in our hearts, and no matter how hard we try to hide that person they continue to live, and when the time is right God has the power to revive and restore the hopes of the hidden man of our hearts.

When he does resurrect that person he brings life back into him, so he can serve God, God is a God that when he wants us, he only wants, and needs the best of us for his service.

He chooses the one who thinks he or she is not capable of doing anything good or right, or who feels unwanted or unloved. And when we think we are not the best, he knows we are the best, and we are the best for the job he has chosen us to do.

Why do you think God chose Saul Paul to be one of his disciples?

(Acts 8:3) As far as Saul goes, he devastated the church, going into every church house, calling out to the men and women who were Christians, then he put them in prison.

Saul decimated the church, he went into every church, and called out to the men and women that were Christian's, and after they answered him, he put them all in jail.

(Acts 9:1) And Saul, once again uttering from his mouth threats to kill that were targeted towards the Lords disciples, went to the high priest.

Then again Saul spoke from his mouth threats to kill the Lords disciples, then Saul went to the high priest.

(Acts 9:2) And wanted him to give him letters that were written to the houses of worship in Damascus, so the letter's would allow him, should he find anyone who was a Christian, regardless of whether they were men or women, to allow him to bring them back to Jerusalem in chains.

He went to the high priest because he wanted him to give him letters that he could take to the synagogue in Damascus, and once he did this once the letter was given to the high priest it would allow him to put Christians in shackles, and bring them back to Jerusalem, and it did not matter who they were man or woman.

Paul acted like this, and in spite of this God chose him because he knew the true Paul, not the man that was on the earth, he knew the hidden man of the heart. And God knew that Saul was a steadfast man for what he believed in, and he had a great enthusiasm for the work he did for man.

So, God knew if he turned him around, and used him for his purposes, he would get the job done that God needed him to do. Saul was a very well learned man, he was a scholar, and he knew many different languages, and all he used to God's advantage, once Jesus converted him, he brought many souls to Christ, and he was so well learned in the religion of his day.

(Acts 23:6) But when Paul saw that one part of the people were Sadducees, and the other part was Pharisees, he yelled out in the council, Men, and brothers, I am a Pharisee, and a son of a Pharisee: and am of the belief and the resurrection of the dead, and I am being called into question.

But when Paul saw that the people were Sadducees, and Pharisees, he started screaming out in the council, telling them that he was a Pharisee, and he was a son of a Pharisee:

And that he believed in the true God and in the resurrection of the dead, and that his belief in the resurrection was being questioned by the council he was standing before. He knew when he told them he was a Pharisee that he would cause a division amongst them, because he knew their ways.

(Acts 23:7) And when he said that a strong disagreement rose up between the Pharisees and the Sadducees: and the crowd of people divided up too.

When he said that, a powerful argument broke out between the Pharisees, and the Sadducees: and then the people who were gathered there split up too.

(Acts 23:8) Because the Sadducees said there was no resurrection, no angels, and there was no Spirit: but the

Pharisees acknowledged one as well as the other.

The reason for this was that the Sadducees said the resurrection did not exist, nor did angels, and the spirit did not exist either: But the Pharisees believed in one as well as the other.

The Pharisees where Jews, but the Sadducees were not, so they would not have known anything about the Jews beliefs, or even about the resurrection, angels, or the spirit.

(Acts 23:9) Then a great cry rose up, and the scribes who were of the Pharisees' part rose up in opposition, saying, We found no malice in this man: but if a Spirit or an angel has talked to him, let us not oppose God.

Then a loud argument rose up, and the Scribes who were there who were part of the Pharisees' they rose up against the Sadducees, and said, there is no hostility found in this man: but should a spirit or an angel have talked to him, we will not go against God.

(Acts 23:10) And when there rose up a considerable amount of quarreling, the chief captain, was scared that Paul was going to be pulled apart by them, he commanded the soldiers to go down, and take Paul by force from amongst the people, and bring him into the castle.

When they started to argue, the Head Captain, became afraid that Paul was going to be ripped apart by them, so he ordered the soldiers to go down to were Paul was, and forcibly take him from among the people, and bring him into the castle.

(Matt. 16:18) And I am saying to you, that you are Peter, and on this rock, I am going to build my church; and the doorway of hell will not win against it.

I am saying to you that you are Peter, and upon this rock I in the future will build my church; and the gate way of hell will not get the victory against it, because I will defend it.

(Jn. 1:42) And he delivered him to Jesus. And when Jesus saw him, he said, You are Simon the son of Jona: you will be called Cephas, and the translation of this name is, a stone.

And he brought him to Jesus, and when Jesus saw him, he said, your Simon the son of Jona; you're going to be known as Cephas, and the meaning of this name is the rock.

Jesus knew Peter was the rock, and he chose Peter to begin the building of the church at Pentecost because he knew Peter's heart.

As dirty as we may believe we are when we give our hearts to Christ, he makes us white as snow. You can't turn the heart off, and on like a light switch: you can't demand that it be obedient to your demands when you are not God, the owner and ruler of all hearts. Your heart should be carefully guarded.

(Prov. 4:23) Continue to keep your heart with every care, because out of the heart comes the water of life.

Go on protecting your heart with all possible efforts, because from the heart the water of life flows out.

We are to protect our hearts from every evil, carefully, because out of our hearts the water of life flows, and if we want to keep it flowing then we are not to allow anything into our hearts that could corrupt it.

Because once it is corrupted that water will not be able to flow again, until we ask God's forgiveness, and he forgives us and makes it flow again.

(Prov. 23:7) Because as he thinks in his heart, so he is: Eat and drink, says he to you; yet his heart is not with you.

Since the fact is that in his heart, he is what he thinks he is: drink, and eat, he says to you, but his heart is far from you.

Just because someone eats, and drinks with you does not mean he really cares for you, because it is his heart that determines the kind of man he is.

He can do these things with you, and still his heart can despise you because his heart is not the same as yours, his character has a flaw.

(Matt. 6:18) So you do not appear to men to be fasting, but to your Father who is hidden, and your Father, who sees in secret, will reward you openly.

Then you are not to let men see you fasting, only your Father who is unseen should know you are fasting, and your Father, who sees in private, will pay you in a way that everyone will be able to see.

We are not supposed to look like we are fasting in front of men, we are not even supposed to tell anyone we are fasting, only God is supposed to know what we are doing.

And only he can see the secret things of our hearts, and because he can see the secret things in us, he said he will reward us out in the open, because he can see our character.

(Rom. 10:10) Because with the heart man believes to godliness; and with the mouth acknowledging your sins are made to salvation.

It is our hearts that cause us to believe so we can reach godliness, and by using our mouths we let the Lord know we know what sin is and ask to be forgiven for it, these acknowledgments help us to find salvation.

All I speak is from the abundance of my heart, should I stop speaking from my heart, I stop being who I really am.

The heart is the center of your life, should I stop speaking from my heart, I not only deny who I am, but I deny the God of my salvation too. Because of an experience in my past, I was reminded were my heart lies, and that is with God.

(Matt. 15:10) Jesus summoned the multitude together, and said to them, listen to me, and understand:

Jesus called the great number of people together, and said to them, hear me, and learn:

(Matt. 15:11), it is not what goes into the mouth that defiles a man; but it is what comes out of the mouth, that defiles a man,

What goes into a man does not make him spiritually dirty; but it is what comes out of his mouth, this is what makes him spiritually dirty,

(Matt. 15:16-20) Jesus said to them are you still so dull? Jesus asked them: don't you see that whatever enters the mouth goes into the stomach, and then out of the body? But the things that come out of the mouth come from the heart, and these make a man unclean.

Jesus told them are you still so dim? Then he asked them: don't you get it, whatsoever goes into the mouth goes into the stomach, and then it goes out of the body?

But whatever comes out of the mouth it comes from the heart, and these are the things that make a man spiritually dirty.

The definition of unclean is being polluted with evil, and with unclean thoughts, these polluted things that come out of a man are not of God, they are of the world, they are of self, and are not things that make God happy.

God wants us to have love in our hearts, and everything that he is he wants us to have inside of us. He wants us to give the love in our hearts to the people we love, to the people who are a part of our lives. He wants us to give love, even to our enemies.

When Jesus asked them are they still dull? He meant are you still not able to hear me? Do you still not understand what I am saying about what makes a man spiritually dirty?

To be dull is to be spiritually unintelligent, having no spiritual life inside, having no wisdom, being spiritually unimaginative, unable to hear or understand spiritual matters. The bible says that a person is spiritually asleep when they are referred to as being dull.

(Jn. 15:13) Greater love has no man than this, that a man give up his life for his friends.

Stronger love no man has than this, that a man should give up his life for his friends.

Jesus had a great love, we know he did because he gave up his life on the cross for all his people, who he referred to as his friends.

(Jn. 15:14) You are my friends if you do what I command you to do.

Jesus believes that we are his friends, because we do what he directs us to do, we do it because we believe in him. We know that he will lead us in the right direction because he loves us.

WHEN GOD SPEAKS

(Rev. 1:10) I was conversing with the Spirit on the Sabbath, and I was able to hear an unusually powerful sounding voice at my rear, and it's sound was similar to a trumpet.

The Apostle John was talking with the spirit on the day of the Lord, and he was able to hear a voice that was full of power behind him and it sounded like a trumpet.

(Acts 9:4) And he dropped to the ground, then he could hear a voice, that said to him, Saul, Saul, why are you persecuting me?

And Saul fell on the ground, then he was able to hear a voice, Saying to him, Saul, Saul, why do you harass me?

(Acts 9:5) Then he said, who are you, Lord? And the Lord said, I am Jesus who you've been persecuting, it is difficult for you to strike your feet against the pricks.

And then he asked, "who are you, Lord?" the voice said I am Jesus, whom you are trying to hurt: Jesus was telling Saul that the road he had taken was a hard road.

And all the kicking and screaming that he was trying to do would not heal his spiritual wounds (pricks). And that he could not hurt the Lord, no matter what he did.

(Matt. 3:16) And at the time Jesus was baptized, he went straight up out of the water, then looked, and was able to see the heavens opening up to him, then he saw the Spirit of God moving down out of the heavens looking like a white dove, blazing like a fire as it made contact with him.

After Jesus was baptized, he walked out of the water: and when he looked up, he saw the heavens opening up to him.

Then he was able to see the Holy Spirit of God coming down out of heaven in the form of a dove made of burning light, and this light was like a burning fire as it came down to unite with him:

(Matt. 3:17) And turning his eyes to see, a voice came down from heaven, and said, this is my very much-loved son, in whom I am extremely pleased.

After Jesus baptism, a voice from heaven said, "This is my son, whom I love with all my heart, in him I am very well pleased.

(Ex. 3:4) And the LORD saw that he turned to come see, then God called him from the center of the bush, and said, Moses, Moses, and he said I am here.

When Moses went to look at the burning bush, the LORD saw he turned to come see, then God called him from inside the bush, and Moses answer was Here I am.

When Moses answered God gave him directions and answered his questions and told him his plans for his people and also told him that he would be with him and how to use his staff (Ex. 3:7-22).

(Gen. 4:6) And the LORD said to Cain, Why are you angry? And why has your face dropped?

Then the LORD said to Cain, why are you so angry? And why have you dropped your face.

(Gen. 4:7) If you do what is good, wouldn't you be

recognized? And if you do not do what is good, then sin will be waiting at the door. And his desires will be given to you, but you have to restrain him.

Then he tells him if you do what is right, will you not be accepted? But if you do not do what is right, sin is crouching at your door, and his desire is to have you, but you must control him.

And he who desired to have Cain was Lucifer, and the LORD was telling Cain not to give into him, that he needed to deal with Lucifer, so he could stop him from having control over him, by taking control over him.

All through God's word he speaks to men and woman, calling them by their names, him drawling them with his spirit, by the name of the son, in their sleep, and in their waking hours.

Always trying to guide them, and lead them in righteous directions, and in the process making them aware that sin is always stooping at their door; sitting there desiring to have them when really all a man has to do is learn how to be the master of the sin in his life.

And the only way to control sin is to trust, and believe in the master of our lives, and the master who is able to put that sin in its place because he is the true master of sin, and the only one able to destroy it is Jesus Christ.

Needless to say, Cain did not listen to God, and chose to do wrong and he ended up killing his brother, and God avenged his brother because his blood cried out to God because of what Cain did, and because of what he did the earth cursed him.

(Num. 7:89) And when Moses went into the tabernacle

of the congregation to talk to him, at that time he was able to hear the voice of someone who was talking to him from the mercy seat that was on the ark of the testimony, coming from among the two cherubim's: and he did speak to him.

And at the time that Moses went into the house of worship (tabernacle) of the assembly (congregation) to talk to him, he was capable of hearing the voice of a person who was talking to him from the seat of mercy.

Who was on the ark (protection) of the testimony (truth), this voice was coming from between the two cherubim's: and he talked to Moses. The voice he heard talking to him was the LORD's voice.

(Num. 8:1) And the LORD talked to Moses saying,

The Lord spoke to Moses again, saying,

(Duet. 4:12) And the LORD spoke to you from out of the middle of the fire: and you heard the voice of the words, but you saw nothing that resembled (similitude) him; you only heard a voice.

And the LORD talked to you from the center of the fire: you were able to hear the voice of his words, but you were unable to see anything that looked like him; you were only able to hear a voice.

The word spoke is a past tense of speak so this scripture was spoken in the past as we know. So, the Lord spoke to the inside of Israel from the place where he was covered up by the glory of God.

They were able to feel the words, but were unable to see any image of him, and even though they were unable to see him, they were still able to hear his voice.

(Duet. 4:36) Out of heaven he made you to hear his voice, so he could possibly give you instructions: and on the earth he showed you his strong fire; and you heard his words coming from the center of the fire.

From heaven he caused you to hear his voice, so he could give you directions: and so, he could on the earth show you his mighty flame; and you were able to hear his words that were coming from the middle of the fire.

The fire God allowed them to see was his glory, and the Lord Jesus was covered by it. So, this scripture say's, from his resting place he made you understand his language using his abilities, and power, he was able to teach you, giving you knowledge, and directions.

And from his high place on the earth, in his tabernacle, he allowed you to see his outstanding, celebrated glory; and you heard his son Jesus from this place who was covered up by the glory of his Father.

The Lord our God comes to speak to us, because he wants to guide us, and in guiding us he gives us knowledge, and direction, he opens the scriptures to our minds through the Holy Spirit and allows us to see what we are unable to see with our natural eyes, what we can't see if we do not talk with him.

If we do not hear him, if we can't talk with him. If we do not listen to him when he speaks or calls, then what he comes to give our ears, and our eyes, we will not receive.

We were made to hear his audible voice, and at his choosing we are given his knowledge, wisdom, and his teachings.

Because this is the will of the Lord, I just have to say "Thank you" for making me just to listen to you, and your will, I think it is an awesome thing to know that one of the reason's he made use was to listen to him, and to teach us his language, and wisdom.

This lets me know this was something he chose to do for use, and he did not have to do it, blessed be the name of the Lord!

FASTING

Fasting is done to deny the flesh, and when you do this, you are denying the body something it needs to thrive and live, and when you fast; it helps the spiritual man grow, it causes the spiritual man to thrive and come alive inside of you. Also fasting brings you closer to God and it helps to get your prayers answered.

When you fast, you are denying the flesh, and the feeling of it, and when you do this the feelings of the flesh die over time, and when this happens the spirit is able to grow and become stronger as time goes on. Fasting can be done by denying the body food, sleep, or drink, even not having sex is a form of fasting.

(Matt. 4:2) And when he had fasted 40 days and 40 nights, later on he was hungry.

When Jesus fasted for 40 days, and nights, later on he became hungry.

(Matt. 4:3-11) After not eating for 40 days, and nights, when Jesus was done, he was ready to do spiritual battle that concerned the temptations of Satan, and after the confrontation he was victorious. Fasting had strengthened him in his spirit just for this particular fight.

When we fast, we are showing humility in our spirits in front of God, we are presenting ourselves to him in humility, showing him that we are ready to do the will of the LORD.

In doing this we are letting God know we want his will

to be done in our lives, through this we are showing him that we are listening and being obedient to his will. Some can only fast a short amount of time, others can do it for longer periods of time, depending on what fast God has decided he wants a person to do.

(Neh. 9:1) At this time on the 24th day of the month the children of Israel were gathered together, through fasting, and wearing Sack cloth, and ashes on themselves.

On the 24th day of the month the children of Israel came together, and they did not eat any food, and they wore mourning clothes (sack cloth), and put ashes on themselves.

(Est. 9:31) To verify these days of the Jewish holiday Purim in their appointed time, and in agreement to this fact Mordecai the Jew and Esther the queen had ordered them and like they had commanded for themselves and for their children, the things of abstaining from food and crying.

This verse says, to confirm that these are the days of the Jewish holiday Purim, and that this is the appointed time for them to celebrate it, and this is according to what Mordecai the Jew and Esther the queen had commanded the children of Israel to do.

They also had commanded themselves to do this for themselves, and their children, and to do the things that involved not eating any food and crying out to the Lord.

Purim is a Jewish holiday celebrated on Adar 14, that is in February or March, in a leap year, to commemorate the deliverance of the Jews from the massacre planned for them by Haman the Agagite (Esther 9).

(Ps. 35:13) But as for me, when they were sick, my clothing was sackcloth: I humbled my soul with fasting; and my prayer returned into my own bosom.

But for instance, me, at the time they were sick, my clothing was mourning cloths: and I lowered my soul through fasting; and my prayer came back into my own breast.

David was saying that when he prayed, he put on cloths that were for mourning, and though he humbled himself through fasting; his prayers never reached God, they returned to him, going into his chest.

Depending on what one might be going through, or what has happened between God, and the person who is sending up a prayer through fasting, and mourning, God may not receive the prayer one is sending up. In that case the prayer will return to them unanswered, it all depends on the situation, and the condition of the man's heart.

(Ps. 69:10) "When I cried, and humbled my soul with fasting, that was to my shame."

When I cried, and humbled my soul with fasting, that was my dishonor.

A lot of times in the bible when one fasted, and put on mourning cloths, and ashes it was because they had sinned, and they were trying to make amends with God.

They had to admit their fault (reproach) in front of the Lord and make things right with him. In this verse his crying and fasting really was humiliating for him.

(Ps. 109:24) My knees are wobbly through fasting; and my flesh fails from heaviness.

This person's knees were giving way because he was fasting, and his body was breaking down because he was carrying a great weight.

I can only guess that the weight he was carrying was for the sin that was in his body, which may have been the reason he was fasting, I can only guess.

(Jer. 36:6) So, you go, and read from the scroll, that you have written from what I spoke from my mouth, the words of the LORD, speak them into the ears of the people in the LORD's house on the day of fasting: then you will read them into the ears of everyone of Judah who comes out of their cities.

Then you are to go, and speak from the document, that you have written from what I spoke out of my mouth to you, that are the words of the LORD.

Talk about them in the ears of the people inside of the LORD's house on the fasting day: at that time, you will read them into the ears of every person who is of Judah that comes out of your cities.

(Dan. 9:3) And I positioned my face towards the Lord God, to seek the Lord through prayer and petitions, with fasting, mourning cloths, and ashes:

And I faced in the direction of the Lord God, to search out the Lord through prayer, and pleas, with fasting, and wearing mourning cloths, and putting ashes on my head:

(Joel 2:12) So, as well now, said the LORD, you are to turn to me with all your heart, and with fasting, and with crying, and with sorrow:

Then, also at this time, said the LORD, you are to turn to me with every bit of your heart, and with fasting, and crying, and in grief.

We are to turn to the LORD with our full hearts, through fasting, and crying out to him, and giving our sorrows to him, this is what he wants.

(Acts 14:22) Verifying the souls of the disciples, and warning them to go on in the faith, and that we have to through a lot of troubles go into the kingdom of God.

We are to provide evidence of the truth of the lives of the disciples and advise the children to be careful as they go on in the faith and advise them of what we have to go through and that is a lot of tribulations so we can go into the kingdom of God.

We are to research, and examine the words of the bible, and seek out God, so we can ascertain the truth of the courage of the disciples and warn the children to keep on going in the faith.

And make sure they know that we have to go through a whole lot of difficulties, and dangers, so we will be able to enter into the kingdom of God.

(Acts 14:23) And when they decreed them to be elders in all the churches, and prayed for them with fasting, they ordered them to go to the Lord, in whom they had faith.

And when they had ordained them to be elders in every one of the churches, and they had prayed, and fasted, they instructed them to go to the Lord, in whom they believed.

(Matt. 17:14) When they came to were the people were, then came to him a particular man, and then this man kneeled down to him and said,

When they had gotten to where the people were, a specific man came to him, and kneeled down before him, and said,

(Matt. 17:15) Lord, have compassion for my son: because he is insane, and is suffering in mental pain, and very irritated: because he has frequently over time fallen into the fire, and has frequently fallen into the water.

Lord, have mercy for my son: because he is crazy, and does suffer from mental anguish, and is very annoyed: because he has fallen many times over a period of time into the fire, and many times into the water.

(Matt. 17:16) And I have brought him to your disciples, and even they could not heal him.

And I brought him to your disciples, but they could not heal him.

(Matt. 17:17) Then Jesus responded and said, O you who have no faith, and are of a degenerate generation, how long will I be with you? how long will I support you? bring him here to me.

At this moment Jesus replied, saying, O you who have no belief, who are of a generation that has deteriorated, for how long will I be with you? for how long will I have to assist you? bring him over here to me.

(Matt. 17:18) Then Jesus reprimanded the devil; and the devil left, going out of him: and the child was healed from that moment on.

Then Jesus denounced the devil; then the devil left him, going out of him: and the child was restored to good health that instant.

(Matt. 17:19) Then the disciples came to Jesus separately, and said why couldn't we cast him out of his body?

Afterwards the disciples went to Jesus apart from everyone else, and said, how come we were unable to make him leave his body?

(Matt. 17:20) And Jesus said to them, because you did not have faith: because in truth I say to you, if your faith is as small as a grain of mustard seed, you will say to this obstacle, you need to move now to that place over there; and it will depart; and there will be nothing that is impossible to you,

Then Jesus said to them, you were unable to because you did not believe you could: because the truth is that I am telling you, if your faith is as small as a mustard seed, you will be able to say to this mountain, move now to that place over there; and it will leave; and nothing will be hard for you.

(Matt. 17:21) However this type does not come out except through prayer and fasting.

Still this kind will not just come out, they will only come out through prayer and fasting.

This scripture told me that there are different kinds, classes, and categories of demons. And that this demons intentions was not to leave a person's body. Jesus made it known that fasting and prayer are what are necessary to get this type of demon to leave a person's body, fasting does serve a very important purpose.

(Lk. 2:36) And there was a woman whose name was Anna, she was a prophetess, and she was the daughter of a man named Phanuel, who was of the tribe of Aser: who was very old, and had lived with her husband 7 years, being a virgin when they married.

Anna was a woman who was a prophetess, who was the daughter of a man named Phanuel, she was of the tribe of

Aser, Aser was one of the sons of Jacob.

Jacob was the father of 12 sons who are referred to as the twelve tribes of Israel in the Old Testament. She was an elderly woman, who had lived with her husband for 7 yrs. Before his death, and she married him when she was just a virgin.

Anna was a woman who spoke for God, she was the daughter of Phanuel, and Phanuel means "face of God". She was of a remarkable maturity, and had lived with her husband perfectly, for 7 yrs. The word perfectly meant that she was an admirable wife, she was a good wife to him all the years they were married.

(Lk. 2:37) And she had been a widow for about 44 years, who never left the temple, but served God with fasting and prayers day and night.

She was a woman who survived her husband, and she never remarried, and she never left the house of the Lord, she obediently worked in the service of the Lord, denying herself, and spiritually communicating with God day and night.

She served him as she denied herself, talking to him, connecting with him, she devoted her entire life to him, being a faithful woman of God. She was able to see, and recognize the importance of fasting, and prayer that she needed to use in her unity with him.

And she was able to recognize how important it was to follow God's directions in her work for the temple. Her faithfulness is one of the reason's she was mentioned in the bible, had she been unfaithful there probably would not have been any mention of her.

Not only had she been faithful to God, but she had been a faithful wife to her husband at a time when divorce was going on, she remained a faithful woman of God, keeping her husband in prayer in front of God.

The word fasting has the word fast in it, the word fast means quickly, and swiftly, this is what God does, when we fast God moves swiftly on our behalf, when we fast, and pray this shows the Lord how dedicated to him we truly are.

And by showing him our dedication he moves quickly to answer our prayers. Fasting also causes our spirits to take flight in the spiritual realm, causing our spirits to move in a way that they are unable to move in the natural realm of the earth. Because in the spiritual we do not have these fleshly bodies weighting us down, so we can move more swiftly in the spiritual realm of heaven when God has control of us.

We may not be able to see this movement, but God sees it, this is why we must believe in the unseen God, and if we believe in him, then we will be able to believe that we are in his kingdom moving around because of the Holy Ghost that is in us, it makes it possible for us to be moving in the heavens, while our bodies are still walking in the earth, because we are just as spiritual as he is.

YOKES

(Lk. 14:19) And someone else said, I have brought with me 5 oxen who are harnessed by a yoke, and I will go to take care of them: I pray that you will excuse me.

And somebody else said, I brought with me bulls that are harnessed by a yoke, and now I will go take care of them: I ask you to excuse me.

(1Tim. 6:1) Have as many of those who serve that can, who stay together in servitude (yoke) to rationally think that their own keepers deserve to be honored, in this way the name of God, and his instructions won't be talked about as being wicked.

Permit those who are servants, and who cling together in an obedient relationship, to believe that their own owners do deserve all honor, so, the name of God, and his doctrine will not be spoken of as being evil.

This is talking about the relationship between a servant and their master who owned them in ancient times. And that the servant was to show respect to their owner's because this was something they owed them.

Because the person who professed to believe in the Father and the son were not to disrespect God by disrespecting their master. So, no one would talk badly about Gods teaching's, so their actions would not reflect back on God and what they had been taught by him.

(Acts 15:5) However certain ones of the denomination of the Pharisees did rise up who thought to say, it was a necessity for them to be circumcised, then they ordered them to continue keeping the law of Moses.

Some of the Pharisees wanted the disciples to follow after the law of Moses and demanded that the disciples be circumcised. This was the ceremonialism that they followed after, but God would not allow this to happen to the disciples.

Circumcision was in the Old Testament under the Law of Moses, we are no longer under the Law, we are under grace, under Jesus. In today's times circumcision is done for the health of the male child, not because of the Law of Moses.

(Acts 15:10) At this time why are you trying to test God? Trying to put a binding (yoke) that will dominate the disciples around their necks, that not even our fathers or we were able to bear.

At this time why do you try God? By trying to control the disciples using cruel force, this was something that none of our fathers could deal with, and neither are we able to deal with it either.

The yoke of ceremonialism is a yoke religious people like to put on people when they come in contact with their religious ways. and they think everyone is supposed to carry this heavy load because they say so.

Ceremonialism attempts to load a believer down with all kinds of rules, and regulations that were not even written in the bible to be done in the church or in the service of the Lord.

And if they are calling themselves following the word, they are trying to follow it with no Holy Spirit dwelling on the inside of them, therefore they cannot follow it.

Ceremonialism can also turn someone who believes

they are walking correct into one of the biggest demons ever created on the face of the earth, and the person would never know it because they would believe what they are doing is right.

Read about Saul in the book of Acts if Jesus had not knocked him down, and changed his life how many more Christians would have died beyond those he killed prior to his conversion? But God saved them by saving Paul, and taking the ceremonialism out of Paul's life, changing him; and then God used him for his purpose.

(2 Cor. 6:14) You should not be badly matched (unequally yoked) when in a relationship with someone who does not believe: because what involvement does holiness have with unholiness? And what friendship does good have with evil?

You are not to be in an imbalanced relationship with someone who isn't a believer: and the reason for this is that holiness, and unholiness can't have an association with each other. What involvement does holiness have with sin?

We who are saved are not to enter into a relationship with someone who is not, because we are believers in Christ, and the other person who we are trying to be with is not. They are not because they are still in a relationship with the ruler of their flesh, Lucifer.

And we are in a relationship with Christ, and the two can't get along with each other. There is no relationship between holiness, and unholiness, and good, and evil could never get along, evil would hate good, and the good would suffer for not listening to God.

Sometimes we think oh, they are the way they are, but I can fix them, wrong we can't, only God can, and it is pointless to be around someone who God has not dealt with, and think that if we stay eventually, they will treat us right.

Wrong again, because while you are staying with them, and believing God is working on them you are still in the line of fire, and you will still be mistreated by them.

And there is no guarantee that if you stay with them for years that they are ever going to change, because there are some out here who truly do change, and there are others who never do. And the only one who could know who will truly change, and who will not, is the Lord God almighty.

(Deut. 28:48) Because of this, you are going to be a servant to your enemies that the LORD is going to send in your direction, while you are hungry, and while you are thirsty, while you are naked, and while you are in want of everything: and he will put you in bonds made of iron (yoke): and put them around your neck, doing this till he kills you.

Because of this, you are to be a servant to the enemies that the LORD will send to you, doing this while being hungry, thirsty, and naked, and while you are in want of everything: and your enemy will put you in shackles of iron (yoke) that will be put around your neck, and he will do this till he has killed you.

Moses was talking to the children of Israel telling them what would happen if they did not listen to the word of the LORD. And he was letting them know if they did not obey God's word that they would end up being slaves to the enemies that the LORD would send to them, and they would be hungry, thirsty, and naked.

And they would be wanting everything, and their enemy would put them in chains (yoke) of iron that would be put around their necks, and he would let this go on until their enemies had kill them.

(1 k. 12:4) Your father made our service hard: and because of this you should make the hard service of your father, and

his hard to bear load (yoke) that he put on us, a bit easier then we will serve you.

Your father made our service painstakingly hard: and now as a result of this you need to make this painstaking service that your father made, and his burden that we had to carry that was strenuous that he placed on us, a bit easier, then we will serve you.

Jeroboam and the congregation of Israel went to talk to Rehoboam, and told him, Your father made our service to him laborious: and because of this they wanted him to make the laborious service of his father, and his hard to bare burdens that he placed on them, much easier, and if he did this, then they would be happy to serve him.

(Isa. 9:4) Because you have slain the persecutor (yoke) who caused him trouble, and slain the power that rested on his shoulder, and the authority of the one who drove him like a slave, as was done in the day of Midian.

Due to the fact that you have defeated the slave driver who was the cause of his difficulties, and have crushed the power that he was carrying, and the power of the person who drove him like he was a slave, as you did in the days of Midian.

It was God who did all this, freeing Israel from the one who was causing them pain and making things difficult for them. God took down the power that Egypt was carrying, and he crushed the power of Egypt who ran Israel like they were slaves.

He put an end to this Egypt's reign of terror, destroying the yoke of oppression that Egypt had on them, this happened in the days of Midian, were Moses came from to deliver the children of Israel out of Egypt.

(Lam. 1:14) The restraints (yoke) of my sins stay

connected by his hand: they have been coiled around me, then they come up my neck: and he caused my power to stop working, then the Lord handed me over into their hands, from whom I cannot rise above.

The shackles (yoke) of my sins are restrained by his control: his sins loop around and come up my neck: he has stopped my strength from working, and it was the Lord who handed me over into my enemies hands, and because of who I am, I am not able to get out of this situation.

This tells me that it was God who was using this person's sins against him by making it into his yoke, to keep him under control. His sins curled around his neck, and was made to go up, and around his neck: and it was God who made his strength leave him.

Then the Lord handed him over into his enemies hands, and because of who he was, he did not have the power to climb out of what he was going through. This means because he was a man of sinfulness, he couldn't undo what God had done to him.

(Lam. 3:27) It is good for a man to hold up under the pressure (yoke), that is on the inside when he is young.

It is good for a man to remain strong beneath the influences that life puts on him, his strength comes from inside of him when he is young.

This is a heavy burden that a young man has to carry when they are trying to mature, trying to find their way through life, not sure about so many things, and trying to learn how to follow God.

(Matt. 11:29) Take my servitude (yoke) and let it completely touch you, come to know of me; because I am calm and humble in my heart: and you will find rest to your heart.

Take my service, and let it fully influence you, come to know me; because I am tranquil, and have humility in my heart: and rest you will find for your heart.

We must voluntarily hold onto the service that we do for Jesus, and when we hold onto it, it will produce a powerful effect in us totally, then we will come to understand him; and the reason we will come to understand him is because he is peaceful, and humble in his heart: and he will help us find rest in our hearts.

(Matt. 11:30) Because my agreement (yoke) is not hard, and my load is of little weight.

Because my agreement (yoke) with you is not difficult, and my duty holds very little weight.

God is humble, submissive, yielding, and unpretentious, plain, and quiet in the secret place of who he is. We should expect to reach him through our efforts of searching him out.

We should decide to say yes to the agreement that he has made with us, and we should agree to take on the duty of serving him. As well, we should try to locate Jesus relief, because his relief is our freedom from anything that wearies, or tries to trouble us, or anything that tries to disturb us mentally and spiritually.

Should we do this we will be able to find peace for the nature of who we are. Jesus' agreement (yoke) is not hard or difficult; it requires no great labor or effort. It is free of pain, discomfort, worries or cares, his yoke gives us ease and comfort, it is not restrictive, and is very comfortable. And his responsibility is to his radiant light that is the Holy Spirit of his Father, who is our God.

THE PROMISES OF GOD

A promise is an expressed assurance, that something will or will not be done. When it is done, it is an indication of a future realization, it is a promise from God of something that will truly be fulfilled, because he is a God that makes sure that what he promises will be done.

(Heb. 6:13) Because when God made the promise to Abraham, he could not swear by one greater, so he swore by himself,

When God made his promise to Abraham, since there was no one greater for him to swear by, he swore by himself.

He said, "I will surely bless you, and give you many descendants. "And so, after waiting patiently Abraham received what was promised. Men swear by someone greater than themselves, and the oath confirms what is said, and puts an end to all arguments.

Because God wanted to make the unchanging nature of his purpose very clear to the heirs of what was promised, he confirmed it with an oath. God did this, by two unchangeable things, himself, and Jesus, in which it is impossible for God to lie, so we who have fled to take hold of the hope offered to us may be greatly encouraged.

We have this hope as an anchor for the soul, firm and secure, it enters the inner sanctuary behind the curtain, where Jesus, went before us, and has entered on our behalf. He has become a high priest forever, after the order of

Melchizedek.

(Gen. 14:18) And Melchizedek who was the king of Salem took out bread and wine: and he was the priest of the greatest and strongest God.

And Melchizedek who was king of Salem took bread, and wine out: and he as well was the priest of the Most High God.

This Melchizedek came many years before the son of God, he was the king of Salem, and the word Salem means peace, so he was the king of peace. And he was a priest of the excellent, and morally powerful God.

(Ps. 110:4) The LORD has sworn, and will not regret it, You are to be a priest forever who would come later, who will be made following after the peace of Melchizedek.

The LORD did swear, and will not apologize for it, you are a priest always, who would come in the future following in the peace of Melchizedek.

The LORD made an oath, that he would not take back, that his son Jesus was to be a priest forever, though his son would not come into the earth until a later time, and he was to move in the same direction as the king of Salem.

Melchizedek was that king of Salem (Peace), so he was the king of peace, and Jesus was made the prince of peace.

(Heb. 5:10) Called for by God to be a High Priest who will come later and follow after Melchisedec.

Called having the spirit of God in him, a High Priest, who would come later, being put in a place that would make him come next in line after Melchisedec.

God called Jesus to come out because he needed him to take ownership of his people, so he made him a high priest who would appear much later in time than Melchizedek did, and he would be made in the same spiritual form, that Melchisedec was, even though Jesus came into the world over 400 yrs. after Melchisedec did, he was still made to be like him.

Now then there was a promise made to Abraham by God this promise was made at a time when he, and his wife Sarah had no children, and where in their old age, and had probably come to the point in their lives that they did not believe they ever would have children.

And Sarah felt she was beyond her years for having children., yet God said to him that he was going to bless him with many descendants, and Abraham waited patiently for the promise God made to him to be fulfilled, and God did fulfill it by blessing Abraham, and his wife with a child though she was in her old age.

God gave her the strength to conceive a son, and the strength to give birth to Isaac. God also gave Abraham another blessing, when he made that promise to him, he told him to look up in the sky when it was nighttime, and told him to count the stars, then God told him his seed was going to be as many as the stars in the heavens.

(2 Cor. 1:20) Because all of the promises of God in him are yes (yea), and in him so be it (amen), to the glory of God, and he will be near us.

Due to the fact that every one of God's promises that are in him are yes, and it is so, glory be to God, and he will be close to all of us.

What he uses to help use connect with each of his spoken promises in Christ, is not only yes, but also in Christ, he uses it is so and so be it (Amen) to speak to us too.

These words are to the honor, and great praise of God, and God uses us as a way of communication. We are what he uses to convey his promises in Christ, because we are able to communicate his promises. He uses his yes, and his so, and his so be it, he uses his honor, and his glory towards those he wants to know him, doing this through us. And while he is doing this, he continues to remain very close to us.

(Heb. 8:6) But now hath he obtained a more excellent ministry, by how much also he is the mediator of a better covenant, which was established upon better promises.

But now he has gotten a more outstanding ministry, and through this ministry he is the negotiator of a much better agreement, that was permanently put in place on more excellent promises.

But at this time, he has come into possession of a ministry that is much more superior, and the evidence of this is how important it is, it is important because he is the person who brought about this much better agreement (covenant), that was founded on much better promises.

But at the present time Jesus has come into possession of something that is of great importance, and that is a significantly large number of true believers, who are very important ministers and who are very important to him.

And Jesus is the representative, as well as being the person who has interceded for a much more upright conditional promise. This promise was founded, proven, and shown to be truly honorable, and a very important announcement was declared, this being a promise from the Father.

This more superior announcement means it was something that was very necessary and was clearly spoken of as being something that was very important to God.

(Deut. 12:20) When the LORD your God expands your borders, like he has promised you, and you will say, I will eat flesh, because your soul longs to eat flesh; you will eat flesh, whatever your soul desires.

At that time the LORD your God will make your borders expand, as he has promised you, and you will say, I am going to eat meat, because your soul longs to eat meat; you may eat meat, and anything your souls desire.

In (Deut. 12:20) the Lord has promised to enlarge the borders of the children of Israel, the word enlarge means that he planned to increase or expand. And borders means boundary, this means that he planned to take the borders off of the people's minds, so their thoughts would no longer be limited, and nothing would be impossible for them.

If they thought they wanted to eat meat; he told them they could, just by thinking about it, and that they could have anything that they desired in their souls to have, just by thinking about it, their minds would no longer be limited in what they were able to think and believe they could have.

(Deut. 6:2) That you might fear the LORD your God, to continue in every one of his permanent rules (statue), that I have commanded (command) you, you and your son, and your son's son, every entire day of your life; and so, your days could possibly be made longer.

That you may be afraid of the LORD your God, to keep going on in every one of his rules that have been put in place, that I have ordered you to, you, and your son, and your son's sons, to do this each, and every day of your lives; and so, your days can maybe, be made longer.

The original word in this verse was statue and this word means permanent rule, and it means that his statue was a permanent rule that was established by the Lord to govern his people.

And the original word in this verse was command, and it means authoritative order, so this authoritative order was given by God who is the one who has authority, and control over his people. He gave this order to them so they and their children's days would be longer on the earth.

(Deut. 26:18) And the LORD has taken responsibility (avouched) for you on this day, so you will become his odd people (peculiar), as he has promised you, and you should continue in all of his rules.

The LORD has assumed responsibility for you today to be his special people, as he has promised you, and then you will have the use of every one of his commands.

The original word in this verse was avouched, and it means to assume responsibility, and to make a frank acknowledgment, so he is saying he assumes responsibly for you, and is making a frank acknowledgment of you, and is saying to you this day that you are to be his.

And the original word in this verse was peculiar, and it means a special people of God's own possession, just as he promised, and it also means an odd people.

(2 Chr. 21:7) Nevertheless, the LORD was not willing

to wipe out the descendants (house) of David, because of the agreement that he had made with David, and the fact was that he promised to give a light to him and to his sons forever.

However, the LORD will not destroy the house of David, because of the promise, he made with David, and he promised to give a light to him, and his sons forever.

God promised to give a light to David, and his son's forever, and that light he promised was Jesus Christ. The word house in this scripture means family, ancestors, and descendants, and that is what sons are, so the Lord said he would not destroy David's descendants because of the agreement he made with him.

The word forever in this verse means the light Jesus will be giving the descendants of David, the light that God promised them forever, that means it would never come to an end. The light he gave was the promised light, of the Holy Ghost, and his descendants were the sons, and daughters of God through the one who was seated on the throne of David forever, Jesus.

(Acts 2:33) Because of what took place Jesus is actually on the right side of God, in his elevated position, and I have been given by the Father the promised Holy Ghost, this is what he released and sent out, this is what you are now able to see and hear.

The outcome of what happened is that Jesus is now really on the right side of God, in his exalted place, and I've been given by God the Holy Ghost that he promised to send back, this is the Holy Ghost that he gave up, and ordered to go out, this is what you are looking at now, and what you are listening to.

In this verse Peter is speaking on the day of Pentecost, and he is letting everyone there know what had actually taken place that day.

He let them know in this verse because of what had taken place with Jesus Christ dying on the cross, he was now seated on the right side of God in his promised position, and that the Father had fulfilled his promise, and had sent the Holy Ghost back to them like he said he would.

And letting them know that the Holy Ghost had been set free, then he told them that what they were able to see and hear was the Holy Ghost speaking to them that day through Peter, and the disciples.

God fulfilled his promise that day, he fulfilled it hundreds of years after he made the promise, and he is still fulfilling his promises even today, in our time, what a mighty God we serve.

ROOTED & GROUNDED

(Eph. 3:16) So he could give you, in conformity to the wealth of his glory, to strengthen with power by his Spirit on the inside in the inner man:

So then, God will give to you, that which is of the nature, and the valuable source of his greatness, this will make you strong with the power of his Holy Spirit, that will be on the inside of you, in the inner man.

God will give you the Holy Spirit who follows after, and does everything that Jesus instructs it to do, it is Jesus who is the valuable source of Gods greatness (glory).

And it is Jesus who will strengthen you with the power of his Holy Spirit when he places it on the inside of you, and when he puts it in you, it will be placed into the deepest secret places of your inner man. Into the parts of your mind that have as of yet not been fully discovered by any man, and only the Lord is able to find it.

(Eph. 3:17) So, Christ can live in your hearts through faith; so, you will have life being secured in place (rooted), and your feet on the ground (grounded) in love.

Then, Christ will be able to live in your hearts through your belief in him; then you will have life, and be secure in a place of safety, and your feet will be planted firmly in the land in love.

Then Christ will live inside of your hearts because of

your faith, and then you will have life in a place that is safe, because you will be established in the principles, and the ideas of the Lord God almighty.

And you will be able to spiritually stand (rooted) having your feet firmly planted in the land (ground) of heaven, and you will be able to show that you have good spiritual sense, and you will be able to make good sound judgments (grounded) in the love of Jesus Christ.

(Eph. 3:18) Perhaps you will be able to come to grasp the idea with every child of God, what is the scope, the direction, the intelligence, and the objective.

Then maybe you will be able to comprehend with every saint what is the effectiveness, the guidance, the intellect, and the goals of God.

Then you will be able to see as every child of God comes to see the things that the Holy Spirit is capable of. You will come to see its purpose, its functions, its potency, its capabilities, its usefulness, how compelling it can be, and how ready to serve the Lord it is.

You will come to see its leadership, how it council's us, how it cares for us, how it gives us advise, how it assists us, how it teaches us, and how it helps us. You will come to see how intelligent it is, and how knowledgeable it is.

How it acquires knowledge from the Lord, how it understands everything the Lord tells it, how perceptive it can be, and you will come to understand its spiritual mind, how it thinks, its reasoning, and how it celebrates the Lord.

You will come to understand what its aim and objectives are as far as serving the Lord, and how it does all it has been tasked to do, and how it has come to finish the work that God has sent it out to do. Through Jesus Christ, and the Holy Spirit all of God's intentions are fulfilled, these are his goals.

(Eph. 3:19) And to come to understand the love of Christ, that surpasses all intelligence, so you may be filled up with all the riches of God.

So, you will come to be familiar with the love of Christ, this love that goes beyond all earthly knowledge, and this is so you might be filled up with every one of Gods treasure.

Then you will become comfortable with the Love of Christ, this love surpasses all the abilities for learning that the earth has to offer you, this is that way, so you will have the chance to be filled up with all of Gods overflowing fullness in the spirit.

The word root is the bottom of a tree that plants itself in the dirt at the beginning of the plant's life cycle, it is what gives the plant its first foundation to grow right. It also helps the plant to stay in place, and the roots also provide the plant with food, water, and nutrients.

The reason I have been teaching and explaining the word in the way that I do is because I am trying to build a firm foundation in Christ Jesus in the way the Lord wants it to be built. And in order for someone to have a true understanding of the word they must learn about the roots of the word of God.

Some people show up one day, and say they are saved, and living for God, but have neglected to learn about him, or have either not been taught properly or gave no effort in seeking God out for themselves, so they could have his guidance. They neglect to learn about Gods fundamentals, so they never develop the roots that they need to serve him in the way he wants, them to serve him.

A person like this will never be able to stand, and serve God in spirit and in truth, and until they learn about him in the way he wants them to, they will never be able to, because they will not be able to serve who they don't know. And one can't know him until they get to know him in the way he wants them to.

We are the trees he grows, and in order for us to grow in the way he wants, our roots have to be fed by God with his water, the water of life, and his food that is the word of God. As a matter of fact, we are grown by God, so the fruit we produce should be of God, and it should please him.

(Gal. 5:22) But the fruit of the Spirit is love, happiness, peace, going through troubles, kindness, strength, and having faith,

But the fruit of the spirit is love for others, joyfulness, peace, enduring troubles patiently, being gentle, being good, and having faith.

When we grow as God's trees the fruit that should grow from us should come from the Holy Spirit, after it has been planted in us. And the fruit that we should bear because of the spirit would be love, and this love should be a love that we should have for each other, and other people who may not know our Father.

We should have joy in our hearts because of our Father and be calm inside knowing that he is with us, we should be able to hold up under immense pressure in hard to bear times, and still be able to show kindness to others, being strong, and courageous, and be able to still have faith in God.

(Gal. 5:23) Humility, and self-control, and fighting against this particular Spirit, there is no ruling for it.

Being quiet in our characters and having self-restraint: and trying to be contrary to this, there is no rule for it.

We should be humble, and be able to control our selves', and if anyone tries to fight against the specific nature of the Holy Spirit, they need to know that God has given no command for them to do so.

When we are growing out in the world the fruit, we produce is unacceptable to God, because it's not what he says is fit for someone who is holy.

(Gen. 4:1) And Adam knew his wife, and she got pregnant, and brought forth Cain, then she said, I have received a man from the LORD.

And Adam intimately knew his wife, and she became pregnant, and she gave birth to Cain, and then she said, I have gotten a man from the LORD.

(Gen. 4:2) And once again she brought forth his brother Abel. And Abel was a shepherd of sheep, but Cain was a farmer of the earth.

And once more she gave birth to his brother Abel. And Abel was a shepherd of sheep, but Cain farmed the land.

Cain grew fruits, and vegetables; while Abel was someone who kept sheep.

(Gen. 4:4) And Abel, brought the first (firstling) to be born of his sheep and the plumpest (fat) of them. And the

LORD recognized (respect) Abel, and his offering, he found Abel, and his offering to be worthy:

And Abel, brought to the Lord the sheep that had been born first, who had filled out, because they had been well fed. And the LORD accepted him, and his offering, and he found Abel, and his offering to be deserving of his attention (worthy).

Abel gave God the firstlings of his flock, and the fat of it, and the Lord honored Abel, and his offering. He gave God the first (firstling) of what was born of his flock of sheep, and he gave God the best, and the plumpest of his sheep. He did not give him the last or the sick, and he gave it to him from the very beginning, he did not pick out what he wanted first then gave God what was left over. And because Abel did this God respected his offering and acknowledged him.

God respected his offering because Abel put God first, and acknowledged him as God of his life, giving him what he asked him for.

(Gen. 4:3) And in the course of time it happened, that Cain brought to offer to the LORD the fruit of the ground.

Over a period of time is when, Cain brought an offering to the LORD that was of the fruit that came from the ground.

(Gen. 4:5) But to Cain and his offering the LORD had no consideration (respect). And Cain was terribly angry, and his face dropped (fell).

But Cain's offering the LORD did not want it, as a matter of fact he did not even bother to consider it. Then Cain actually got angry that his offering was not excepted by the LORD, and he dropped his head.

Cain did not give God what he wanted, he gave God of what he grew from the earth and what he wanted to give him, and this displeased God, and God did not have respect for Cain, or his offering.

God was a God of fleshly sacrifices, he could not have fruits and vegetables for a sacrifice to him on his altar, he did not want earthly things sacrificed to him.

So, Cain got angry, and his face fell, and he became sad, then God asked Cain why was he angry? God warned him about the devil being at his door waiting to destroy him.

(Gen. 4:6-7), But Cain was not a man who was learned in the ways of the Lord, but Abel was, his heart loved the Lord, Cain's did not.

If Cain had listened to God, then he would have given God what he asked for. But he did not listen to him, because he was not of him, Abel was, God raised Abel, he was grown in Gods garden, nurtured by God, loved by God and he loved God back, Cain didn't.

He was a tree that God had planted by his roots, by his river, while being raised those roots took deep hold in the land of the Lord.

So deep that when his brother killed him out of jealousy, Abel's blood that was his life knew to cry out with a voice to the one who had raised him, loved him, and nurtured him. His life cried out from the ground where it had spilled, and the earth opened up her mouth and swallowed it up.

(Gen. 4:10) And he said, what have you done? The voice of your brother's blood cried out to me from the ground.

Then he said, what did you do? Your brother's blood cried out to me with a voice from the ground.

So, God, and the earth dealt with his brother after Abel's physical body had died, there is nothing like being rooted, and grounded in the word of God.

(Gen. 4:11) And at this moment you are cursed, the earth has cursed you, that has opened her mouth to take in your brother's blood from your hand.

Now you have been cursed, because the earth cursed you, the same earth that opened her mouth, and drank your brother's blood from your hand.

These roots also help us to stand when the pressures of life come in like a flood, and where we probably would have run away in fear, these roots say no way am I going to run. I am going to stand still till the God of my salvation comes, and pulls me out of this distress, and makes things better for me.

Writing helps me to have a focus on Jesus, if a person has one thing in life that they adamantly focus on when things begin to go wrong or seem as though they are getting the best of them, if they turn their focus back to that thing that has been their focus, it helps to ground them, and things become so much clearer once again, for me this is the LORD Jesus Christ, he is the one who helps me focus.

The word says that we as children of God are to be rooted, and grounded in the word, that means when people come our way or spirits try to sway us from the truth, we will stand firm, being unmovable on what we believe, and who we believe in.

Because our roots have grown and are planted so deep in the soil of the Lord, and his word that when these things come our way, they are not strong enough to pull us out of whom we are planted in, and they can't remove who God has planted inside of us, Jesus Christ.

SOWING SEEDS

What makes a person able to be a good teacher is his or hers life experiences and what they have been taught by God. Whether they are good or bad experiences, God has placed them in our lives so when we are older, we will be able to teach the next generation what not to do on their way to where we have already been.

And what to do on their road to becoming what God wants them to be. But if we close up or shut down who we are on the inside because we are embarrassed or ashamed of what we have accomplished in this life when it comes to our experience; we are no longer a benefit to someone that we've come across who needed to hear what we suffered and went through on our way to becoming what God had planned for us to be.

We can't be unfair to God by shutting it all up, and not sharing it with others, I had to face this fact years ago when I came across a young man that I cared about, who was showing me things from his point of view, and I enjoyed seeing things from his perspective.

But when I should have shown him life from my perspective, I couldn't because before I saw him again, I had closed down my heart, and it would not open up to him, and I didn't know how to get it to open.

This happened because I refused to tell anyone who I really was, and so when God brought this person into my life, again I could not tell him who I was in Christ because God closed that door in me.

You know I remember that God said if you be ashamed of me, I'll be ashamed of you, and I see it as when I refused to tell anyone who I was, it was like saying I was ashamed of God, and so after I refused to admit who I was, when I wanted to admit it, God would not let me do it.

You know sometimes good people make bad mistakes; it does not mean they are bad people, sometimes mistakes are made unconsciously. A good person is always a good person in spite of the mistakes, or hurtful things they have said or done.

Those who love teach correction, and do not force it, and if correction is not taught then a child will not learn or grow, into the person God wants them to be, and know they can become. That is why when a parent does not correct, God comes in, and does the correction himself, his rod no man's hand can stop, and no man can take it from him.

(Prov. 3:11) My son do not despise the discipline of the LORD; nor be tired of his punishments:

My son do not hate the correction of the LORD, and do not get tired of his punishments:

(Prov. 15:10) Punishment is sorrowful to him who has forsaken the way: and he who hates to be reprimanded will die.

Punishment causes grief to a man who has abandoned Gods way: and he who despises being reproved definitely will die.

Being reprimanded definitely will make a man cry who has turned his back to the Lord. And any person who hates to be taught what is right will eventually be wiped off the face of this earth.

(Prov. 23:13) Don't refrain from punishing a child because if you touch him with a rod, it won't kill him.

Do not hold back when it comes to punishing a child: because if you strike him with a stick he won't die.

This was written in the word long ago, today in the world we live in striking a child is not accepted. Me, when I was raising my children, I would tell them I was going to let life be my rod of correction. And life did strike them, and it did correct them in a way I never could, because God is life, and he did it for me.

(Isa. 55:11) So my word will live that has gone straight out of my mouth, and it will not come back to me empty, but it will do what I have sent it out to do, and it will fulfill what I want it to, that which will make me happy, and it will grow in the thing I have sent it into, to do so.

God's word will be alive after it has gone out of his mouth, and it will not come back to him having nothing in it, and it will accomplish what God has sent it out to do, and it will carry out what God wants it to do. And what it does do will make God happy, and his word will grow in the thing he has sent it out to grow in.

God's word does God's will, because God has instructed it to; that it will do. God's word is a living seed that the Lord releases directly from the inside of his mouth.

He is making it known that this seed will eventually come back to him, but when it does it will be fully mature, and not be empty in what he released it to do, and it will do what he commanded it to do, and it will do it because what it is sent to do will please the Lord.

It pleases the Lord when his seeds grow and mature in the thing he sent it into to do so. The thing he is referring to is the body of flesh his spirit must go into, and live inside of, to bring spiritual life to a man. To God our flesh is a thing, an inanimate object, that has no spiritual consciousness, to him it is dead in sin, and death is all that comes out of it, until he plants his seed in it.

(Mk. 4:14) The gardener (planter) put the word in the ground. The gardener who planted the word was God, the word was the seed of God.

The gardener puts the seed in the earth. The gardener who plants the seed is God, and the seed is the word of God.

(Mk. 4:15) And these are those near the pathway that was to one side, where the word is planted; but when they heard it, Satan comes quickly, and takes the word away that was planted in their hearts.

These are the people who were closest to going down the road that would take them in the direction of the Lord, that only went in one direction, who were set apart from the rest of the people; these were believers.

And the word was planted in them, but when they heard it, Satan moved in very fast, and removed the word from them, that had been planted in their hearts.

(2 Cor. 9:10) Now he who ministers seed to the Sower does both minister bread for your food, and multiplies the seed you have sown, and does increase the fruits of your righteous behavior;)

At this time, he who is the administrator of the seed, he is the one who provides the seed to the one who will plant it, and at the time he is doing this he is also providing nourishment that is a particular kind of nourishment to you, then he multiplies the seed you sowed, and he makes the fruit's of your righteous deeds grow and become many.

Now the source from the beginning is God who gives the

Holy Spirit to us, so he can be introduced by the planter, who is Jesus, and it is he who supplies the spiritual nourishment to you so you will be able to multiply what he has put in you; by planting it into other believers, and he will multiply what is unable to be seen with the natural eye, that is the product that makes your character spiritually right in godliness.

This thing that is unable to be seen is the Holy Spirit who is His seed, the Holy Spirit can't be understood by the sense of touch, and it can't be physically touched, and it is a being that has no physical substance.

In other words it has no physical body like these bodies of flesh that we walk around in, it does not have one until we believe in Jesus, and when God is pleased with our prayers to him, that is when his Holy Spirit gets to come, and live inside of us, and when it does that's when it gets a physical body to live in, and the only one who can touch the Holy Spirit at all is God, we can only be touch by it.

The Two Seeds

(1 Pet. 1:23) Being born once more, not of a seed that can become corrupted, but one that is not able to be corrupted, being created by the word of God, who lives and remains forever.

It is essential that we are born in the spirit again, being made anew, by being born a second time in the spirit. This second time was put in place because of a prior encounter that caused us to be corrupted by sin that entered into the Garden of Eden through Adam & Eve.

This second creation of man was done to make us in a way that would deny the seed that had no value, this seed had a flaw in it, it caused changes in our spirit man. This seed caused us to decay, wither and die, it was a seed that lacked principles and it didn't do what was right, this seeds father was Satan himself, this seed didn't belong to God.

The seed God was creating was to be of the highest qualities, it would not be lacking in any of Gods spiritual qualities, or his gifts or his riches.

This would be a seed Satan would never be able to destroy, this seed was created from the son of God, who is the living word, Jesus Christ. Jesus, the one who is life, is also the one who will continue in his position, sitting on the throne, in his place as the King of kings.

(1 Pe. 1:24) Because all flesh is like grass, and all the glory of men is like the flowering of grass. The grass withers, and

the flower of it falls away:

Due to the fact that everything that is flesh is considered to be like grass, and all the greatness of men is like the flourishing of grass. The grass shrivels, and the flower of it drops off of it:

This statement is a representation of the life of man, the grass has a speedy destruction because blades of grass are small, and weak, and beneath the beaming rays of the sun they shrivel and die.

In the presence of God men are the size of a blade of grass, should a man have ever been placed in the palm of Gods hand in these fleshly bodies, this is the size a man would be compared to him.

The beaming rays from the sun that withers us are the hardship's, trial's, and temptation's that plague us all the days of our lives, putting pressure on us to push us to our bodily demise. The greatness of man, that is like the grass, and his prosperity all fades away, man loses all the freshness of their youth, because of sin, and because man ages.

The word wither means to decline, and dry up, and when his life withers from the original sin, sin causes the body to decline, and dry up, it also steals the youth of the body, and as the body descends under the pressure of sin it withers back to the earth from where it came.

It's existence in the earth comes to an end, eventually not being remembered anymore by any man, becoming just a memory to some, and over time not even that to others.

(1 Pe. 1:25) But the word of the Lord endures forever, and this is the word that through the gospel, is made known

to you.

Still the word of the Lord Jesus Christ continues to live on forever, this is the word that was opened up to you that is called the gospel, and because it was opened, you have been given the privilege of being allowed to come to know him, and it continues to be resistant to the sin of this world even till this day.

Being patient as it has been enduring for a very long time, it has done this because it has been alive for a very long time. Suffering a lot without giving into what has caused it's suffering, and it will do this forever.

As well this is the written testimony of the Lord who was mentioned previously through his teaching's, his living declaration being put inside of us through the sermons of his Apostles.

(1 Jn. 3:9) Whoever is born of God does not commit sin: because his seed remains in him: and he can't sin,

Anyone who is brought forth of God does not do the deeds of sin: because God's seed stay's inside of him: and because it does, he is unable to sin.

Anyone born of God will not do the deeds of sin, the reason for this is because what God has created in the man will always continue in the man, God has placed it in the man to preserve him to himself. After this he comes to be a living being in the spirit because God has put his Holy Spirit inside of him by causing him to be born again.

The word brought means God caused the man to come to him, and the word forth means to come out. So, God caused the man to come to him, and made him come out of sin, the word anew means the man was given a new form, and new mannerisms, this was away for him to begin his life again, to have a new life.

    Because of all God did for man he no longer had to be a servant to sin, and now he could walk in the newness of the life God has given him through the seed that serves God's purposes, the seed that is known as the Holy Spirit.

THE HOLY SPIRIT, CHRIST JESUS

Earlier today I saw the word holy in my mind, and I knew the meaning of the word without picking up a dictionary. The meaning God gave me was being whole, and we become whole when we are reunited with God.

He is the true God who lives in his spiritual fullness. The meaning of full as far as God goes is that he is not defective, he is perfect, and he is capable of having everything that he does in an abundant supply, no part of him is lacking in anything spiritual.

Jesus is not limited in his power either, and he has all rights, and privileges that his Father has. Also, God has taught me that he has created wonderful mind's in all of his children as well.

And they can do great things for us only if we allow God to train them to meditate on him, and Jesus Christ, and permit him to give spiritual wisdom, and knowledge to us, and refuse earthly knowledge because it only destroys.

(Phil. 1:6) In this way, speaking of your faith could come to accomplish a purpose by you admitting to each, and every good thing that is on the inside of you that is in Christ Jesus.

So, through us talking about the belief that we have in Christ, our talking about him accomplishes a purpose, and this purpose is by our talking about him, it shows that we acknowledge all the good things that have been put inside of us, since we came to be in Christ Jesus.

(Ex. 31:3) And I did the work of supplying him with God's Holy Spirit, putting it on the inside of him, and I supplied him with the teachings of wisdom, putting it inside of him too. And putting inside of him spiritual intellect and putting inside of him different types of skills.

God has done the work of filling a man on the inside whose name was Bezaleel the son of Uri, who was the son of Hur, of the tribe of Judah with the Holy Spirit.

And when he did, he gave him his godly teachings, and his spiritual intelligence, and gave him all forms of spiritual skills so he could do the metal work he needed him to do for his tabernacle and do it in the way God wanted him to do it.

(1 Cor. 15:48) As is the natural, alike are those who are natural: and as the heavens, alike are they as well who are from the heavens.

Just as the world is natural, so are those who are of the world: and just as the heavens are, so are those who are from the heavens.

Basically, in this world we have a physical existence, and this is called a natural existence, and anyone who follows after the desires of their physical form, that is also called their natural form they will not know anything about spiritual matters.

Because they will not have come to know the spiritual matters of God and they don't want to know. But in the heavens one who serves God in the heavens and those who serve him on earth, they are spiritually alive.

And all who are part of heaven, and who live in heaven have a spiritual existence and do not want to know anything about the desires of the physical body, they do not follow it, nor do they want too.

(1 Cor. 15:49) And because we have been made in the form of the natural, we will as well be made in the form of the heavens.

And because we have been born in the form of these earthly bodies, we also will be born in the form of the spiritual beings of heaven.

(Lk. 24:49) And look, I am sending what my father promised to you: still you are to wait for me in the city of Jerusalem, till you are provided with the powerful force that will come from on high.

Jesus told his disciples that he was going to send the Holy Spirit that his Father had promised: and they were to still wait for him in the city of Jerusalem, until they were armed with the strength, and the power of the Holy Spirit, that was going to be coming down out of heaven from on high.

(Jn. 21:18) Really, really, I say to you, when you were young, you clothed yourself, and walked to whatever place you would: but when you become old, you will extend your hands out, and a different person will cloth you, and take you to whatever place you would not go.

Truly, truly, I am telling you, when you were young, you dressed yourself, and you walked to wherever place you wanted to go, but when you get older, you will put out your hand, and another person will dress you, and lead you to wherever place you will go.

The person who would dress them and lead them to where they would go would be the Holy Spirit. It would take them to the places that the Father would tell them to go. It would guide them there and they would walk in it's courage, and it's mind set, they would not have any fear while they did the work God needed them to do, because the Holy Spirit would be their protector.

(Jn. 20:21) Then Jesus said to them once more, Peace be to you: as my Father has sent me, in the same way so do I send you.

Then Jesus said to them again, peace be with you: like my Father has sent me to you, I do the same, go, I am sending you.

(Jn. 20:22) And when he said this, he exhaled on them, and told them, You accept the Holy Ghost:

And just as he said this to them, he breathed on them, and said to them now, you receive the Holy Ghost.

(1 Cor. 12:3) This is why I gave you spiritual comprehension, in order that you will know that any man who talks through the spirit will never call Jesus unholy, and no man can call Jesus Lord, but by the Holy Ghost.

This is the reason I gave you spiritual knowledge, so you will know that no one who is speaking by the Spirit of God will ever say, "Jesus is cursed", and no one can say, "Jesus is Lord", except by the Holy Ghost.

No man who has the Holy Spirit will ever say Jesus has a devil, and they will not say that Jesus is a devil. Anyone who does say these things does not belong to God.

(1 Cor. 12:4) At this time there are different kinds of gifts, but the same Spirit.

There are different types of gifts, but they all come from the same Holy Spirit.

(1 Cor. 12:5) And there are different kinds of services, but the same Lord.

And there are different types of works that are done for God, but they come from the same Lord.

(1 Cor. 12:6) There are different types of actions, but the same God causes them to work, all of them inside of all men.

There are different types of functions, but it is the same God who makes these functions work, each one of them inside of every man.

(1 Cor. 12:7) At this time the manifestation of the Spirit is given to all men for it to be a benefit for them.

Now the appearance, and the demonstration of the Holy Spirit is given to all men so it can be a help to them.

(1 Cor. 12:8) Because one gift is given by the Spirit, and it is the word of understanding; but to someone else the word of faith is given by the same Spirit;

Now to one person is given through the spirit the word of comprehension: to another person the word of truth by the same spirit.

(1 Cor. 12:9) To someone else faith is given by the exact same Spirit; and to someone else the gift of spiritual mending; by the exact same Spirit.

To another person belief is given by the same spirit; to another person the gift of spiritual healing; by the same spirit.

(1 Cor. 12:10) To someone else the workings of revelations, to someone else finely sharpened spiritual awareness; to someone else different types of communications; to someone else the gift of being able to convert or decipher and explain

the scriptures of the bible.

To another person the working of miracles, to another person a precisely distinct spiritual mind; to a different person different kinds of languages; to someone else the gift of being able to transform and find out the meaning of the scriptures and being able to make it known in detail what the scriptures are really saying.

(1 Cor. 12:11) But all of these work the one and the very same Spirit, separating to each man freely as he wills.

Still all of these use the one, and the very same spirit, it separates to each man with a purpose as he has decided to. Basically, God disperses the Holy Spirit to each individual child of God with a purpose in mind as he has chosen to do, he has a reason and an aim for doing this.

The Holy Spirit is the fullness of God in the spirit of his son Christ, and it is his reason for doing what he does, and everything for a totally anointed life dwells in his precious Holy Spirit, and his son is all we need to walk in victory, in the newness of life. To walk in the newness of life is to be guided, and instructed by the recently discovered spirit of Jesus Christ that comes to live, and dwell in you when you accept Jesus into your life.

I say recently discovered because when someone says yes to the Lord, and they receive the Holy Ghost, then to that person it would be a recent discovery. Because when it enters them, it will have found them, and they will have recently found it.

(Lk. 2:40) And the child got older, and became strong in Spirit, and became full (filled) of spiritual intelligence: and the favor of God was on him.

As this child got older, he came to be spiritually powerful in the spirit, and came to be completely filled up with the knowledge of the Holy Spirit, and his Father's favor was placed on him, and this child was Jesus Christ.

(Lk. 4:1) And Jesus having been made full of the Holy Ghost came back from Jordan, and was led by the Spirit into the desert,

Jesus had been filled with the Holy Ghost when he returned from Jordan, being led by the Holy Spirit, and then the spirit took him into the desert.

(Lk. 4:14) And Jesus came back in the strength of the Spirit into Galilee: and the notoriety of him went out throughout all the country nearby.

When Jesus returned, he returned in the power of the Holy Spirit, then he went into Galilee: and rumored reports of him went out over all the lands of the nearby country.

(Lk. 4:18) The Holy Spirit of the Lord has united with me, and since he has empowered me with the Holy Spirit to declare the teachings of the gospel to those who are in need; he has also sent me to make those healthy whose hearts have been broken, to declare deliverance to those who have been imprisoned, and to recover the eyesight of those who lost theirs, and to give liberty to those who have been spiritually destroyed,

Because the Holy Spirit of the Lord has joined with Jesus and has ordained him to announce the teachings of the Father to those who are in need; to let people know he was sent to end the conflict between Lucifer, and God, and to restore man to God.

Through this Jesus helped to mend all wounded hearts,

and announces deliverance from the power, and penalty of sin to those who have been kept in a spiritual prison, and he was to give back the spiritual vision of those who had no sense of spiritual sight, and who are in today's times spiritually pressed, and squeezed so the flesh will die, and so the Holy Spirit might live.

Jesus was chosen by divine appointment by his Father to deliver the doctrine, and the commands of his Father to those who lacked in spiritual wealth, to restore, and make spiritually healthy those who were burdened with grief, sorrow, and disappointment.

To deliver, and set free from moral corruption, and to regain mental understanding for those who have no thoughts of what is spiritual or what is spiritually right, and to restore those who are broken.

And to free from imprisonment those who had been put into a spiritual prison, and because of this being done they were in terrible pain, especially psychologically, and to deliver all this effectively in a specific period of time.

(Lk. 4:33) And in the Jewish house of worship there was a man, who had a spirit of a dirty devil, and who cried out with a loud voice,

And in the synagogue, there was a man that had a spirit inside of him that was a violent demon, and this demon was crying out very loudly using a loud voice,

(Lk. 4:34) Saying, leave us alone; what have we to do with you? You Jesus of Nazareth? Have you come to kill us? I know who you are; the Holy One of God.

Saying, go away, and leave us; what do we have to do with you? You Jesus of Nazareth? Are you here to kill us? I know who you are; the Holy One of God.

(Lk. 4:35) And Jesus reprimanded him, saying, Hold your peace, and come out of him. And when the devil had thrown him into the center, he came out of him, and did not injure him.

Then Jesus scolded him, saying Stop talking, and get out of him. And after the demon threw him down into the middle of the synagogue, he left his body, and he did not hurt him.

(Lk. 4:36) And they were all greatly surprised, and spoke amongst themselves, saying, What a word is this! Because with a commandment and strength he commands evil spirits, and they leave.

All who saw Jesus make the evil spirit leave the man's body were greatly amazed, and they talked about it amongst themselves, saying What kind of word is this! And the reason for this was they thought with an order, and power he spoke to the evil spirits, and they just left.

The Holy Spirit in Jesus because of the things he was able to say amazed the people, and it testified of itself by the power, and authority Jesus used to cast the foul spirit out of the man.

(Lk. 7:21) And in that same time he healed many people of their ailments, troubles, and sinful spirits; and to many who were blind he returned their eyesight.

And at the same time, he restored the health of many people, healing them of their illnesses, distresses, worries, agitations, and evil spirits; and he gave spiritual eyesight to so many who had lost it. Jesus was not broken or decaying from sin as other men were because he was a spiritual being who was the son of God, and because of who he was, and whose he was, he was able to help all other people.

THE HOLY SPIRIT, AND GOD'S CHILDREN

(Jn. 3:4) Nicodemus asked Jesus, If a man can be born when he has gotten old? Can he go back a second time into his mother's womb and be birthed again?

Nicodemus was asking Jesus; How can man be born after he has gotten old? He wanted to know if a man could go back into his mother's womb again and be born a second time?

(Jn. 3:5) Jesus responded, Really, really, I say to you, unless a man is birthed from the water, and the Spirit, he is not able to enter into the kingdom of God.

Jesus told him actually for real except a man is born through baptism and the Holy Spirit, and he is given power by the spirit he can't go into the kingdom of God.

(Jn. 3:7) Do not wonder about what I have said to you, You must be born once more.

Don't feel amazed at what I am saying to you, You have to be born over again.

(Jn. 3:8) The wind blows where it pleases, and you hear a sound because of it, but you can't tell from what place it comes, and where it goes: in this way is everyone birthed of the Spirit.

The wind does blow where it wishes, and you can hear the sound that the wind makes, but you can't tell what direction it is coming from, and you can't tell where it is going: this is the way every child of God is who are born of the Spirit.

This is saying that the Holy Spirit is like the wind, you never know where it is going to blow, and you can never hear it coming, and you cannot tell what direction it is going to come from, and you will never know where it is going.

It is an unknown entity that only God knows what it is doing and what it is going to do when a person is to be born again. All that is known is that the person who is to be born again has gained the understanding of what Jesus meant when he said those words.

And they ask to experience being born again, and God gives them what they asked for, and the only time that it is known what the spirit of the Lord is doing is when it enters into a person, and they realize that a change has taken place in them, and they know at that moment that they have receive the gift of the Holy Spirit and they have been born again.

(Jn. 4:24) But do not change, the time has come, and this is the time when the real worshipers will worship the Father in Spirit and in truth: because the Father seeks this kind to worship him.

But don't you change anything, now the time has come, and this is the time when the true worshipers will come, and worship the Father in spirit, and in truth: because the fact is that the Father is seeking this type of people to worship him.

(1 Jn. 3:9) Whoever is born belonging to God does not do the works of sin; because his Holy Spirit remains inside of him: and he cannot sin, because he is born belonging to God.

Whoever God births in the spirit belongs to God, and

they do not display the behaviors of sin; because his Holy Spirit stays inside of them: and they can't sin, because they have been reborn in the spirit, and belong to God.

(Gal. 4:29) But he who was born following the flesh wounded him who was born following the Spirit, still then it is in this time.

But the person who was born walking after the flesh hurt him who was born having the Holy Spirit, as it happened previously it is the same in these times.

It was man who was born walking after the sins of his flesh, and it was sinful man who injured him who was born having the Holy Spirit, the one who had the Holy Spirit, and who was injured was Jesus Christ, and as it happened to him then it is still happening now, today to the true children of God.

(1 Pet. 1:23) Being born once again, but not of a seed that can be perverted, but of a seed that can't be perverted, being birthed again through God's word, that is alive, and will remain alive forever.

Becoming spiritually alive once more, not of a seed that can be led away from what is right, but of a seed that can never do wrong, being brought back to life once again through the word of God, that does live, and will stay alive always.

Man must be born again of the Holy Spirit, and all who are born of the Holy Spirit are like the wind, no one knows where we will blow, and when God sends us to speak the word, we speak it in the power and authority that he has given to us.

Also, only the true worshipers will be able to worship God in the power, and honesty of his spirit, and because we are able to do this the Father makes it his business to seek us out and makes sure that we his children will worship him.

Our Father is a spirit, and he makes us into what he looks like by his Holy Spirit, by the Holy Spirit he places in us once he finds us, as we are searching for him. Just as he is he makes us, and only by the mind of Christ can we bow down and worship him.

If he does not create us in his spiritual likeness then we can't have life, or live in the spiritual realm, and we can't worship there in the way God wants us to either, in the way only the true sons and daughters of God can.

BEING PERFECTED IN THE SPIRIT

The other day a woman told me that we are not being made perfect in the Holy Spirit, and that we are not being perfected in love by the Holy Spirit, and that we do not have the mind of Christ that comes from the Holy Spirit, this is not true.

I told her that we did but every time I tried to say something she would cut me off or tried to talk over me. Even when I tried to tell her I was not going to debate with her about it because the word is not debatable, she still cut me off. So finally, I told her I did not believe her, and I walked away.

As I was walking away God said to me the one thing about having faith and believing in him is we all have a choice, and no one can make you believe anything you do not want to believe.

Me, I have believed in God, and his word for a very long time, and have been rooted, and grounded in it so long that a person could scream at me for sometime and I know that I am never going to believe what that person is saying to me. She believed she was right because she was the daughter of a minister, but even they can be wrong.

(1 Jn. 4:12) No man has ever seen God at any time. If we love each other God lives in us, and his love is made perfect in us.

No man has ever laid eyes on God at even the smallest time, if we have compassion for each other, God will live, inside of us, then his love will improve us, bringing us nearer to his spiritual perfection on the inside. God's love is what makes us better people when we truly turn our lives over to him.

His love is able to make us into the type of person we may have once thought we could never be, or the type of person that we always wanted to be. Still, we serve a loving, caring, and powerful God whose personality in the Holy Ghost is able to create a new man in us, and perfect that man through the love we have for him.

(1 Cor. 2:16) Because who has understood the thoughts of the Lord, so he might direct him? But we have the thoughts (mind) of Christ.

Because who has come to understand the thinking of the Lord, so the Lord could give them directions? But we have the mind of Christ. so, we are able to think like him.

Who can grasp the ideas, and the thoughts of the Lord, so the Lord might be able to give him instructions? We are able to grasp his thoughts, and his ideas because we have his mind since the Holy Spirit has it too and is living inside of us.

I have seen many people who have not been raised in the word and who say they know Jesus, but the word says there are many people out there who claim to know the Lord's word, but they don't.

(2 Tim. 3:5) Having an outer form of Godliness but rejecting the might of it, from this type move around and away from them.

Having an external appearance of devotion but refusing the power of it, from this kind of person go in another direction, and move far away from them.

Having an appearance that looks like they are being devoted to God, and they also seem to have a holy, and righteous character, but are wicked, and disrespectful. They state that the true God is not the true God in how they carry themselves, and in how they oppose him, arguing against his truths.

Not having the ability to do or act on the true Gods behalf, not being able to fulfill his power, having no authority or control in the true spiritual land of God, in the places that God said his children would be able to have authority, being separated from God because they do not walk in his commands.

We are to have a distance from their kind, we are to direct our paths towards God, and away from the paths they have chosen to walk in, keeping in the direction of God, and his heavenly affairs, ever marching to the mountains of the most high God, and away from sin.

(Matt. 21:15) And at that time the head clergy's (chief priest) and scribes had seen the wondrous things he had done, and the children crying in the temple, and saying hallelujah to the Son of David; the clergy and the scribes were resentful and very offended.

Now the head clergy, and the scribes saw the marvelous things Jesus had done, and they saw the children crying in the temple, and the children were saying hosanna (hallelujah) to the son of David; and when they heard this, they became very indignant, and very angry.

(Matt. 21:16) And they said to him, You hear what they are saying? And Jesus said to them, yes; haven't you ever read, From the mouths of babies and infants you have perfected praise?

When the head clergy and the scribe's asked Jesus are you listening to what they are saying? Jesus said to them, yes; haven't you carefully looked at my Father's word, and seen from the mouth of the innocent, and those who drink milk God has excellent praises (Ps. 8:2).

Those who drink milk they are absorbing the word of God by the Holy Ghost, and the Holy Ghost drinks, and enjoys it, and gets nourishment from it, and by taking in this milk, this milk helps to stop a man's soul from being spiritually thirsty, no longer is it in the dry condition that sin put it in.

The milk of the word is what a newborn baby in Christ drinks, and it helps to mature them on their way to eating the meat of the word, this meat is referred to as the deeper things of God's word.

And the Father creates a perfect praise in us, and when we his children, open our mouths at his insistence to give him praise what comes out is something that can only be expelled by the power of the Holy Spirit praising its Lord along with us, and praising him with a praise that is perfect in the ears of our Lord.

And what makes it perfect is the fact that it is going up to the throne through the power of the Holy Ghost, and God is well pleased to receive the true honor, and glory that comes from the mouth of one who is newly spiritually born, having the Holy Spirit on the inside of them.

(Heb. 10:14) Because he has by one sacrifice corrected forever those who are holy.

Because his purpose was through one sacrifice to be able to correct forever the people of God who are Holy, and he has corrected them forever.

So, in this verse God's perfection was in the fact that Jesus sacrifice healed us, and spiritually corrected us eternally. His perfecting is a process that goes on always, it never ends, and this process is only for those who are his Holy people.

Now, those who have chosen to walk against the will of the Lord, the perfection created by his great sacrifice will do nothing for them; you must be chosen by the Lord.

(1 Jn. 2:5) But whoever keeps his word, inside of him the real love of God is made complete in them: by this we know that we are in him.

From another point of view whoever takes charge of the word, tending to it, and adhering to it, in him in truth, and with confidence, the love of God will make him fully skilled, and mature in the spirit, causing him to be spiritually complete, and finishing his transformation in God. This means we become aware with the spiritual senses, and with the spiritual mind, and we come to know that we belong to the Lord.

VENGEANCE BELONGS TO GOD

(Ps. 105:12) At this time, they were just a small number of men; yes, a very few in number and outsiders were in them.

In this time, they were a small amount of men; yes, there was hardly any of them, and there were people with them who were not of Israel.

(Ps. 105:13) At this time, they went from one empire to another, and one realm to another that was of other people.

And in this time, they were moving from one kingdom to another, and one royal domain to another, who were of a different people.

(Ps. 105:14) He permitted no man to do wrong to them: yes, he reprimanded kings for their benefit.

He did not allow any man to do anything wrong to them: yes, he rebuked kings for their sakes.

(Ps. 105:15) He said, do not put your hands on my consecrated ones, and do not harm my prophets.

He said, do not touch my dedicated ones, and do not hurt my prophets.

When the children who were of Abraham's seed went from one nation to another and went to other kingdoms and other people God did not allow any man to harm them: yes, he corrected kings on their behalf; saying, do not touch my holy people, and do not harm my prophets.

He took good care of his people Israel then, and he takes good care of his people Israel today, his word has not changed, and his love for us has not changed either. He is the same today as he was yesterday because he is an unchanging God, and he is the God who protects us.

(Rom. 12:19) My greatly loved, do not take revenge yourselves, but to some extent giving priority to anger because it is written, Revenge is mine; I will repay says the Lord.

My cherished ones, refuse to exact revenge yourselves by inflicting pain in return for the pain another has caused you, but in some degree yield to anger, and overcome it, so it can serve its purpose. This matter was mentioned before, and the works of revenge belongs to the Lord, it is in his power to choose to return a reward to the unjust, giving them the compensation that they deserve, the Lord made that clear.

(Ps. 94:1) O LORD God, to who revenge belongs; O God, to who revenge belongs, make yourself known.

O LORD God, to who vengeance belongs to: O God, to who vengeance belongs to, show yourself.

The "O" in this verse is the writer showing pain for what he had to go through, and he is longing for the Lord to come. The word "to" in this verse means the writer is wanting the Lord to come in his direction, wanting him to come to do what he does best.

Because it is his will to inflict his brand of revenge, the revenge that belongs only to God so he can give to those who mistreat, or abuse those who belong to the Lord. The writer desired that God would exact his justice, he yearned for the Lord to show himself strong on the side of his chosen child.

We do not have to take revenge or try to right the wrongs

that are done to us because there is one who sits on his throne who sits high, and looks low, who sees all, and knows all. One who is mighty, and powerful, and able to do above, and beyond all we could ever expect, hope, or imagine. We serve a God who truly loves us, and he will do anything for those who truly love him.

In 1983, I was in the spirit, and someone I knew at the time, pulled a gun out on me because he was trying to stop me from leaving him. I looked at him and smiled, then I laughed, then I told him well if you kill me, I would just be getting to God sooner than I expected to go.

But you, you will have to answer here, and then you will have to answer there. So, if you do not intend on using that gun, then you need to put it back where you got it from, so he put it back in the holster, and left. That day I was not afraid because I knew that this person was not coming after me, he was coming after the Christ that was in me.

And me standing up in the confidence of the Holy Spirit that day even if he had shot me, I would have been alright because I would have been with Jesus, that is the kind of faith God wants us to have in him, that no matter what we go through for his sake, no matter what harm anyone might do to us or try to do to us, when we trust him, we can go through anything.

This truth was evident in the New Testament scriptures, when you see what it has to say about the people who were killed for their belief in Christ Jesus, who were called martyrs. This is the kind of faith the Lord Jesus wants us to have in him, we are to be willing to give our lives for him.

Whether it is through being physically killed, spiritually killed, or loosing every material thing that you have accumulated on this earth, home, children, and family. All of this is something that has caused you a lot of pain, and you know it because of the suffering that you went through, and you experienced for Jesus Christ sake, showing your willingness to go through the test for him.

God allows us to go through things so he can raise his hand to right the wrongs that were done to us, and so he can teach us from the things we have had to go through and use us to teach others how to go through the pains of what we have already had to suffer.

Today I thought because I trusted him, and allowed him to take revenge on my behalf, I am alive today to tell the story, there are many people who have stood in my shoes and are not here today to tell their story.

I praise God because of the words of wisdom that I spoke to that person that day, and I would not have been able to speak those words had I not known him. I praise God because he protected me that day, and he protected me because I trusted him, and I trusted that he would take revenge for me, because he never fails.

HOLINESS IS A LIFESTYLE

I can tell you why God does not let us do things he doesn't want us to do, because to serve God, to live for God is a way of life. And what he tries to teach us is that he does not want us to commit any action that is a sin before him once he cleans us up. He wants us to do what is pleasing in his sight, not what is pleasing to our flesh. His ways are not our ways, and his thoughts are not our thoughts.

(Isa. 55:8) Since my way of thinking is not your way of thinking, nor is your way my way, said the LORD.

Because the way God thinks is not the way man thinks, and the way man thinks is not the way God thinks, said the LORD.

There is a way that seems right to a man but in the end, it leads to destruction. And without holiness, no man will see the Lord. In order to be with the Lord when they leave here, they have to live, and be holy as God says they must be.

That means learning Gods ways, and his commandments, and the only way to live holy is to allow the Holy Spirit to do the living in you, and for you. That means no cussing, no lusting, no lying, no stealing, no deceptions, no envy, and none of the other sins that man commits. And you will not do these things because the Holy Spirit won't let you.

(Heb. 12:14) Seek after peace with every man, and seek

holiness, if a man leaves this out, they will never see the Lord:

We are to search out peace with each, and every man, and we are to search out holiness, if a man tries to find God, and leaves out searching for these things, then he will never ever see the Lord:

(Deut. 5:33) You will advance in all the ways that the LORD your God has commanded you to, so you may be able to live, and so it might be well with you, and so you might extend your days in the land that you will live in.

You will move forward in all the directions that the LORD your God has ordered you to, because in moving forward in his directions you will be able to be alive, and so it might be good with you, and so your days could be stretched out in the land that you will be living in.

When we obey his commands we will have life, wellness, prolonged days, and we will live in the land that the LORD has given us, these are what he has promised us.

(Deut. 8:6) Then you will keep the commands of the LORD your God, to walk in his conduct, and be fearful of him.

At this time, you will continue to follow in the directions of the LORD your God, to proceed in his behaviors, and you are to be scared of him.

The LORD God wants us to continue in his commandments, and he wants us to walk in his actions, and he wants us to have a fear of him that will make us look at him with awe, and deep respect, and he wants us to love him, and serve him with our whole hearts.

(Deut. 28:7) The LORD will make your enemies who rise up against you to be struck down in front of your face: they will appear coming out against you from one direction and run away from in front of you, fleeing in seven different directions.

The LORD will cause your enemies who get up to go against you to be knocked down before your face: your enemies will show up trying to approach you, and trying to come after you to fight you, coming from one way, and then they will run away before you, going away from you in seven other directions.

(Deut. 28:9) The LORD will put you in place as a holy people to himself, as he has made an oath to you if you will uphold the commands of the LORD your God and walk in his ways.

The LORD will put you in your proper position as one of his holy people, and he will do it himself, because he has made a promise to you, and he will do this only if you side with him, and honor his commandments, because he is the LORD your God, and you must continue to walk in his plans, not your own.

(Deut. 32:4) He holds the position of the Rock, whose efforts are excellent: because all his ways are judgment: and he is a God of truthfulness and he has no sin in him, just and righteous is he.

He continues in the position of the Rock, and his achievements are wonderful: and they are wonderful because every one of his ways are in demonstration of his power, and intelligence: he is a God of faith, and what is right, that is who he is.

Him being the rock means that he is solid, strong, tough, and hard, he is unmovable, and unshakable. And this is the rock that came to be the stone that the builders rejected.

Haven't you ever read of this in the scripture: the stone the architects (builders) denied, and did not know, has at this time come to be the chief corner stone:

He is the firm foundation, dependable, and unchanging. He labors for us, he is a problem solver, and his efforts bring results on our behalf, and are correct, exact, and flawless because his directions come from his wisdom.

He is a God who really is spiritually alive, who is real and has no evil or injustice in him. And he is the keeper of truth, and what is real, who is guided by truth, and reason, who is accurate, and honest.

Holiness is a lifestyle, like marriage is a lifestyle, it is something each person who says yes to Jesus chooses to live when they choose to say yes to him. And it is a choice that can't be taken back once the agreement is made with him, you have to go forward, and if you look back you will be considered unfit for God's kingdom.

Joseph who was the son of Jacob was put in prison, and he did not sin against God, he continued to believe in the God he served. He trusted God completely, and in spite of all he suffered his faith continued to be in God.

He did not act like the men he was imprisoned with, and because he did not behave like them, his actions, and his behavior let everyone know who he had meetings with, who he was, and who he served, and that his God was the true God.

He was Gods earthen vessel, and he represented God on earth in front of the Egyptians. He was so faithful to God and was such a faithful servant through all his trials, and hardships that God positioned him to become father and overseer of not just Israel but over all of Egypt, and God rewarded his faithful one.

Joseph lived a lifestyle of holiness before the Egyptians, and his brethren who he showed forgiveness to for the sins they committed against him, by selling him into slavery, God rewards faithfulness, and he rewards us for living a holy lifestyle.

(Mk. 12:10) And have you not read this scripture; the stone that the builders rejected has become the chief corner stone:

The stone, Jesus who was rejected by the Jews (the builders) has now come to be the chief branch (corner) and foundation (stone): this means he came to be the leading member, and founder of the house of God.

(Rom. 12:1) I implore you then, brothers, by the blessings of God, that you offer up your bodies to be a living sacrifice, holy, and worthy to be accepted by God, because this is your honorable service.

I eagerly beg you, and because of this, brothers, in view of God's mercy, to volunteer your life, and surrender it as a means of gaining something more desirable, sanctified, and connected to God which is pleasing to him; this is your wise, and fair duty to be used by God.

(Rom. 12:2) And do not become like this world: but you are to be changed by the restoring of your mind, that you might be able to show what is the good, capable, and perfect, will of God.

Refuse to live, with the nature of one who has the character of this world, who has the attitude, and practices of the societies of the earth. You should be against these practices; you should change in condition, nature, character, and appearance through your thoughts, being restored, recreated, and regenerated, being brought back to your original spiritual condition, the condition God intended for us to be in.

So, your purpose will be to confirm the true nature, and identity of the pure, upright, and unblemished pleasure, and purpose of God.

We are to go after peace, and accept it as a guide, and we are to let it lead us, we are to accept its authority, and know that everybody in the Lord should be accompanied by it. They should also come with sanctity, and godliness.

And if sanctity, and godliness are not with them, or if its lacking in them, after it has been made clear that holiness is something that is required, being talked about before in this chapter. Everyone who chooses to live without holiness will be refused entry by God into his kingdom, and then they will be denied by him.

And they will never be able to have any visions, or be able to see him, and they will never be able to come to know him in the spirit. One who does not live holy will never get the chance to see him, his kingdom, or get to come to know of any of his holy things, these are the requirements of God, you must live a holy lifestyle.

(1 Pet. 2:6) For this reason as well, it is included in the scriptures, Look, I have placed in Sion a chief corner stone,

selected, and valuable; and he who believes on him will not be thrown into confusion.

It has been written in the scriptures that God has put in place in Zion a chief branch (corner) and foundation (stone): that has been chosen, and who is worthy; and anyone who has faith in him they will not be thrust into a state of confusion. And again, this branch and foundation is Jesus Christ and there is no confusion in him.

FRIENDSHIP

Today as I was riding in my car the word friendship came to my mind.

(Prov. 17:17) A friend loves at all times, and a brother is brought forth because of hardship.

A friend loves all the time, and a brother is born when he goes through difficulties.

(Prov. 18:24) A man who has friends needs to show himself to be friendly: and there is a friend who sticks closer than a brother.

A man that has friends needs to show himself to be a friend: and there is a friend who stays closer than a brother, and his name is Jesus.

(Ecc. 4:9) Two are better than one, because they have a good reward for their labor.

Two people are much better than one person, and the reason for this is because of the work that they will do together, and the work they do together will be the cause of them having a worthy reward coming to them.

This verse makes me think about that before the Holy Spirit came, we are one person alone, but after the Holy Spirit comes, we are 2 persons serving the Lord as one, and because we have chosen to work as one, we are worthy enough to receive a reward from the Lord because of the work that we do together.

(Ecc. 4:10) Because if they fall, the one will pick up the other: but trouble is to him who stands alone when he fails; because he has no one to help him up.

Two are better than one because if either of them falls down, one can pick the other one up; but distress will come to him who stands alone especially when he fails; because there will be no one there with him to help him up.

When a man has the Holy Spirit should he fall, the Holy Spirit will be there to help the man up, but hard times will come to the man who has no spiritual help, and times will be even harder when he falls; because he will fall alone, and there will be no Holy Spirit to help him up.

(Ru. 1:16) And Ruth said, do not ask me to leave you, or ask me to go back and stop following behind you: because wherever you go, I will go; and wherever you lodge, I will lodge: your people will be my people, and your God my God:

Ruth asked her mother-in-law not to ask her to go away from her, and she did not want her to ask her to stop following her: because she had a friendship with her, and she wanted to go wherever she went, and she wanted to live where she lived, and she wanted her mother in law's people to be her people, and her mother in law's God to be her God.

(2 K. 2:2) And Elijah said to Elisha, stay here, I am requesting this of you, because the LORD has sent me to Bethel. And Elisha said to him, because the LORD lives, and because your soul lives, I will not leave you. So, they went down to Bethal.

Elijah, and Elisha were good friends, so when Elijah requested that Elisha stay where he wanted him to, because he was on his way to Bethal as the LORD had sent him there,

Elisha said with an oath, that as God lives, and because Elijah's soul lived, he was not going to leave Elijah, and he went down to Bethal with Elijah. He was willing to follow Gods directions with Elijah, even though the directions were not given to him, he supported Elijah, and the work he had to do for God, because they were friends.

(1 S. 20:17) And Jonathan was the reason that David spoke a solid oath once again, and his reason was that he loved him: because he loved him like he loved his own soul, and they were good friends.

Jonathan made David swear again that he loved him: because he loved him like he loved his own soul. He was steadfast, and faithful because he loved David. To be steadfast, and faithful is to be consistent; it is a quality that causes us not to change, we don't change because we have chosen to stand on the faith that we have in the love that we share with one another. These two depended on each other and they trusted each other, this is what real friends do, and this is what God wants us to do when we believe in him.

(Jn. 15:13) Stronger love has no man than this, that a man set down his life because of his friends.

Greater love no man has, unless he does this, that he gives up his life for those who mean something to him. Doing it for those who are linked to him through the love that the man has for them, he is their friend, and one who cares for them, Jesus did this for us.

(Jn. 15:14) You are my friends, if you do whatever I ordered you.

You are my allies (friends), so long as you do whatsoever, I command you to do.

You hold this position of friendship, that has been given to you, long as you do the works of the Father, no matter what Jesus asks you to do.

(Jn. 15:15) From now on I do not call you servants; because the servant doesn't know what his lord does: however, I called you friends; because all things I have heard of my Father I have made known to you.

From now on, I call you, not as ones who are servants, a servant is not aware, and doesn't know the affairs of their master. And because he is not aware he will not understand the true nature of the matters of his Lord, and all he does.

I acknowledge you; love you and called you friends, and I have received everything of the Father because I listen to him and then I have told it to you.

I give you the understanding of the truth of it all. And I do this until it is unable to be removed from your mind, then you will know the truth of it, and take it in, and you should know that you are not servants who work under my directions, you are my friends.

A servant is someone who serves his master, working under his directions, they attend to the master's needs, and they wait on him. Before Jesus took possession of us, we presented ourselves before him to become his servants, as one who needed to learn how to serve, and be an attendant of the Lord. When we came to him, we did not understand the affairs of God, they were foreign to us.

But once we accepted the Lord, and the Holy Ghost was given to live inside of us, then we were no longer servants, but we came to be the loved ones (friends) of God, he loves us enough that he entrusts us with his holy things, and his holy affairs.

His nature is our nature, and his Father is our Father, and because Jesus has taken possession of us, we do not need a master that we have to work under the control of.

So, when the Holy Spirit is placed inside of us it is the agent that teaches us, and we are able to understand all the matters of the Father, the Holy Ghost is the one the knowledge of the Father is fed to through Jesus Christ, and then the Holy Ghost sees the affairs of the Father and shows them to us.

We are no longer servants because before we came to Christ, we were servants to Lucifer, and the sin inside of our bodies, Jesus freed us from that situation, changing our lives, and delivering us from being servants to Lucifer and sin, and then he made us his friends.

The greatest love that Jesus had for us, and that we should have for him is to give up our lives for him because he is our eternal love, and the beloved of God, he is our example because he loved us with such a great love that he gave up his earthly, and heavenly life on the cross for us.

And when he did this, he spoke to the whole human race, and showed them the spiritual authority of the Father.

He laid it down for us, and he made sure that he left behind such a great witness, so we could know and understand why he did this great thing for us at a time when we were truly not worthy.

In our unworthiness he still made a way for us so that when we came to know him, we would be able to learn why God, and our Lord thought we were so worthy of this great sacrifice.

What a mighty, and awesome God we serve that while we were still in our mess, he called us friends: he set it up for us to be called his friends down through the generations and stipulated that this would be only through our obedience to him.

And as he gave his life for us, we are to give up our lives for one another in the love, and worthiness that Jesus Christ showed us as the true sacrifice, and savior of the cross.

His life was worth far more than ours because he was the one true son of God, and still his Father felt his sacrifice was needed for us to live, he shed his precious blood on the cross for an unholy, and wretched people so they would have the opportunity to know through the Holy Spirit what it was to be a begotten son of the Most High God.

Who can say that they have ever found such a great friend as the Lord Jesus? Not everyone can say that they have, but I am glad I am able to say it.

NAMES CHANGED

In the Old and New Testaments names were changed when God's blessings where given, blessings were only given when God's favor was received.

(Jn. 1:42) He delivered him to Jesus. And at the time Jesus saw him, he said you are Simon the son of Jona: you will be called Cephas, that is by interpretation, A stone.

Andrew brought Peter to Jesus. And at the moment Jesus saw him he said that he was Simone the son of Jonah: now you will be called Cephas, when Cephas is translated it means, a stone. From the time that Jesus saw Peter he knew who he was going to be, because he was able to see his future.

(Matt. 16:13) At the time Jesus came into the region of Caesarea Phillippi, he asked his disciples, Who do men say that I the Son of man am?

When Jesus came into the district of Caesarea Phillippi, he asked his disciples, who do men say the son of man is, who I am?

(Matt. 16:14) Then they said, Some say you are John the Baptist: some say Elias; and other people say, Jeremias, or one of the other prophets.

They said to him, Some say John the Baptist: some say Elijah, and others say Jeremiah, or one of the other prophets.

(Matt. 16:15) He said to them, but who do you say I am?

Then he said to them, who do you say I am?

(Matt. 16:16) Then Simon Peter responded and said, You are Christ, the Son of the living God.

Then Simon Peter said to him, you are Christ, the son of the living God.

(Matt. 16:17) And Jesus response to him was, Blessed are you, Simon Bar-Jonah: because flesh and blood has not made this known to you, but my Father who is in heaven.

Then Jesus said to him, divine favor has been given to you, Simon Bar-Jonah: and the reason for this is that fleshly men haven't revealed this to you, only my Father who is in heaven could have told you.

Since God revealed this to "Simon Bar-Jonah" he revealed it to "Hearing son of the Dove", this is what Simon Bar-Jonah means. And symbolically it means "you heard this from God the Holy Spirit, since the dove is the symbol of the Holy Spirit, we could state this, that Simon Bar-Jonah also meant "hearing from the Holy Spirit.

This is saying the only way Peter could have known who he was, was because his Father in heaven gave him the knowledge. This means Peter had gained favor with God because he had connected with him, and because he had Jesus changed his name to Cephas.

(Matt. 16:18) And I say to you, That you are Peter, and on this rock, I will build my church; and the gates of hell will not win against it.

Then I say to you as well, that you are Peter, and upon this rock I am going to build my church; and the gates of hell will not win out when it makes contact with it.

His being called a rock meant he had not spiritually grown,

or matured yet, so, he was not yet the rock that stood in the presence of God when he had been given the knowledge of who Jesus was. But Jesus saw his future, and who he was to become once the Holy Spirit was sent back on the day of Pentecost and given to him.

Then he said that hell's gates will not get the victory over Peter and the church he was going to build, and the gates of hell did not win against his church.

Because when he died on the cross, he broke open the gates of hell, and took back what belonged to him. He took back the keys to hell, and death, and he took back the chosen children of God.

When it said upon this rock, he was going to build his church it meant that Jesus was going to place the Holy Spirit upon the mind of Peter, and when he received it the building of the church would begin. And when the pathways (gates) of hell made contact with it, it would lose the fight, and it did.

Those who belonged to Lucifer, who would come out of those pathways (gates) could not stand up to the power, and authority that Peter, and the disciples would have after Pentecost.

And even in these days, and times they still can't stand up to the power of God, and the children of God because of the Holy Spirit.

(Matt. 16:19) And I will give to you the keys of the kingdom of heaven: and whatever you will hold onto on the earth will be held in heaven: and whatever you will release on the earth will be released in heaven.

And I am going to give you the keys of the kingdom of heaven and anything that you hold onto in the earth will be held onto in heaven: and anything that you let go of on the earth will be let go of in heaven.

If we surrender and let go of the sin that is a part of our lives when we come to Jesus it will be surrendered in heaven, and if we pick it up again it will be picked up again in heaven.

Jesus told Peter that he would give him the keys of the kingdom and these keys would open the doors of heaven that had been locked for a very long time making it impossible for man to get in.

One of the keys that he was going to give to Peter was the Holy Spirit and it would unlock the doors of heaven, and then other keys would be released, allowing the children of God into the holy things of God, and in these holy things the other keys would be found.

This is what gives us entry into the bible and permits us to hear the words of God and helps us to come to know the things of God. These are all keys of the kingdom; these are the things that come from heaven that prior to the Holy Spirits coming we were unable to receive or enter into.

Just before Jesus was crucified Jesus talked about being betrayed and Peter told him that he would not betray him. Then Jesus told Peter before the cock crows you will have denied me 3 times.

When they came to get Jesus to crucify him some people accused Peter of being one of his disciples, and 3 times they accused him, and 3 times he denied knowing Jesus, and after he did the cock crowed, and Peter remembered what Jesus had told him. When he remembered he looked at Jesus, and Jesus looked back at him, and Peter bitterly cried (Matt. 26:69-75).

When it says Peter bitterly cried, it was saying that he had a deep sorrow, so he shed many tears, and when it said the weeping was bitter, it meant he was in terrible pain because he denied the Lord, Peter suffered for his denial of Christ.

Peter thought himself to be unworthy to follow Jesus anymore because he had denied him, so he went back to what he was doing before he met Jesus.

He was probably thinking he has died, and he will not see him again, our thoughts can be so wrong. But one day Peter looked up, and there was Jesus standing on the shore after his resurrection.

He had prepared food for Peter, and the other disciples to eat after they were done fishing; Jesus prepared the table before them. after they were done eating Jesus asked Peter did, he love him?

He asked him 3 times, then he told him to feed his people, and to do the work he was called to do, when the Holy Spirit came back, and Peter received it Jesus prophecy about Peter was fulfilled (on this rock I will build my church) the beginning of the building of Jesus church began with Peter.

Peter was able to be the rock Jesus knew he would be after the Holy Spirit came back on the day of Pentecost, the Rock Jesus, placed the rock the Holy Spirit inside of Peter, and he became the rock the church needed to start building on.

When Peter was given the spirit, it was the finished product of the knowledge he received from the Father, what he suffered for his denial of Jesus, and abandonment of him.

God took all of these factors and combined them with his Holy Ghost on the day of Pentecost, and fully matured Peter causing him to transform into the rock the Lord knew he was going to be.

Peter suffered greatly for the promise of the Holy Ghost, and for the name change he received, and for the gifts God placed on him. When it says placed on, it means the knowledge Peter received through the Holy Spirit was placed in the highest place in his body, and that was his mind.

(Gen. 17:5) Nor will your name be called Abram, but your name will be Abraham; because a father of many nations I have made you.

Neither will your name be Abram anymore, but it will be Abraham: and the reason for this name change is that you are going to become a father of many people, and I have made you this.

(Gen. 17:15) Then God said to Abraham, As for Sarai your wife, you will not call her by the name Sarai, but you will call her by the name Sarah.

Then he told Abraham, and as far as Sarai your wife goes, you will no longer call her Sarai, but you will call her Sarah.

(Gen. 35:10) And God said to him, Your name is Jacob: your name will not be called Jacob anymore, but your name will be Israel: then he called him Israel.

God told Jacob, that his name was Jacob: but that Jacob was no longer his name, and that from that point his name was Israel: then God called him Israel.

The name Israel means "the fighter of God", and "the triumphant with God" and "God contended" and "wrestles with God". Jacob received this name when he wrestled with an angel and refused to let the angel leave until he received a blessing from the angel.

(Isa. 62:2) And those who are not of Israel will see your

righteousness, and all kings your glory: and you will be called by a new name, that the mouth of the LORD will name.

And the people who are not of Israel they will see your righteous behavior, and all the kings of the earth will see your source of honor: and you will be given a new name to be called, and this name will come from the mouth of the LORD, he will name you.

Those who were not of Israel were the gentiles, these were the ones who would see the upright deeds of Jesus, and the kings of the earth would see were his glory came from, these kings of the earth who would see his glory would be the sons and daughters of God.

And he would have a new name given to him, and he would be called by that name, and his new name would come from the mouth of the LORD, he would name him.

(Rev. 3:12) To him who overcomes I will make a pillar in the temple of my God, and he will not go out of it anymore: and I will inscribe on him the name of my God, and the name of the city of my God, that is called new Jerusalem, that comes down out of heaven from my God: and I will inscribe on him my new name.

To the one who defeats sin I will make them a supporting piece in the temple of my God, and he will not go out of the temple anymore: and I will write on him the name of my God, and the name of my God's city.

And the name of his city is new Jerusalem (city of Peace), this is the city that comes down out of heaven from my God: and I will write on him my new name.

The city New Jerusalem is also called the city of Zion.

BEING FORGIVING, LOVE

(Matt. 18:21) At this time Peter came to Jesus, and said to him Lord, how often shall my brother sin against me, and I should forgive him? Up to 70 times?

Now Peter went to Jesus, and said to him, how many times will my brother sin against me, and how many times do I forgive him? Up to 70 times?

(Matt. 18:22) Jesus said to him, I am saying to you, till 70 times: but till 70 times seven.

Jesus told him, I say to you up to 70 times: but up to 70 times 7.

70 times 7 comes to 490 times, this is how many times we are to forgive our brother, but these verses are also telling us that we are to forgive our brother always for the sins he might commit against us.

Really you should forgive all who sin against you, no matter how many times they sin against you. And when you don't forgive it really does not affect the person who has hurt you.

When a person does not forgive it can make their heart uncertain, and the good things that a person's heart could be experiencing are denied, and that person's spiritual growth can be stopped.

And if the grudge you are holding is because of how you were treated in the past by a certain person, and you use it against another person you meet, then you are technically being judgmental of a person who had nothing to do with your past. And you are being judgmental because that is the mind set you had been carrying when you met that person.

You already had your mind made up on how you were going to treat that person when you met them, never giving that person the chance to show who they truly were, putting them in the same mold as the one you believed had hurt you, all because you never forgave them.

(Num. 14:18) The LORD is patient in suffering, and remarkable in his compassion, he forgives wickedness and sin, but his forgiving of them definitely does not clear those who are wrong, going down through the wickedness of the fathers to the children, and to the 3rd and 4th generations.

The LORD holds up under difficulties, and pains, and he is unusual in his love, he is forgiving when it comes to those who are wicked, and sinful.

But this does not clear them of their wrong doings. And this goes through the sinfulness of the father's to the children, through to the 3rd and 4th generation of their children.

The meaning of this verse is the Lord suffers long, and is patient in misery, when he is troubled or provoked. And his love has no boundaries in the scope of its power, and its reach is wonderful, and it tolerates a whole lot.

And because of this it excuses violator's according to what is right. Those violators who commit sin, and who violate the Law of God, and this happens during the time that they are refusing to accept him.

And his love for them and his forgiving them was intended to free the one from darkness, who committed the offense, whose character shows guilt, and who has had the punishment inflicted on them because of the sin of the originator (Lucifer) who brought sin into them in the first place, who has contact with his own children, and his children are the ones who attack and mistreat the children of God,

Just because he does do all of the above his actions don't release them from the blame that they receive for the sins they commit and refuse to repent of.

And this goes down through the evilness of the fathers, to the children, and to the 3rd, and 4th generations of their children, it applies to all.

During the time of Gods patience towards those who violate his Laws, this is the time of his refusal to except the sinful actions that they have committed. He then allows Lucifer, the one who they choose to walk with, and the one who offends God to inflict punishment on them.

Letting him put pressure on them until the 3rd part of them comes out of the darkness from its hiding place, and into the eyesight of God so he can think carefully about them, so he can make a decision about them.

Long as a person is in darkness, and hiding in it, God can't consider them because his position is to refuse to consider a person who refuses to consider him, or he will not consider a person who refuses to give up sin and refuses to love him.

The 3rd part of a man is the mind, a man is made up of body, soul, and mind, and the mind is the part of the man that God wants to come out of the darkness, and freely acknowledge him.

When I say the punishment they receive puts pressure on them, I am saying the punishment puts pressure on them, this pressure forces them to eventually make a decision to either come to God or continue being squeezed like a grape till the day they die, the choice is theirs.

Them being squeezed is designed to destroy them, either sending them running into the arms of Jesus, or if they refuse to change it will continue to put so much pressure on them that eventually they end up physically dying, going back into the ground from were man came.

God's love is so great for us that he forgives us when we have offended him, or forgotten about him, and when we have committed sins in front of him, he still forgives us, still loving us, and this is the reason we are to be forgiving when someone offends us or oversteps the boundaries that we have set up for our lives.

His love can't just cover a numerous amount of sins, but it can reach from one end of the earth, to the other, he can send it further than we could ever imagine. His love is capable of doing so much if we just have faith in him, and believe in his son Jesus, anything is possible.

When man provokes him to anger, he holds his peace, and through his example we should learn to have the kind of self-control that God does, and we should learn how to hold our peace like he does, if God can do it, we can learn from him how to do it too,

When one violates the commands of the Lord, they are put in a certain place in Gods existence, and he does not acknowledge them as far as blessing them, but he still teaches us to pray for them, because the prayers of a righteous man avails much, and that person may not be someone who prays.

(Ja. 5:16) Disclose your flaws to one another, and pray for

one another, that you may be healed. The effective prayers of an upright man avails (availeth) much.

Make your imperfections known to each other, and pray for each other, so you can be healed. Because the powerful prayers of a righteous man are very valuable, and do profit, and serve the LORD very well.

The word availeth means to be of use or value; and to serve. Much in this verse means great in quantity, measure, and importance, it also means a notable thing or matter. So, what it is saying is our prayers hold value, and they are a notable thing in Gods eyes, their value, and quality is in relation to the amount, and the quantity of the prayers that we send up before God, and they are for the benefit of others, and that includes the people of God.

Our prayers profit us and are collectively a wonderful benefit to us because our prayers have force behind them, they have strength, and power, and they serve us well in front of God.

They help us, and helping us is their objective, they are strong in the Lord's presence. Our prayers are a very notable matter when they come up in the presence of the Lord.

A devout petition to God is very powerful, also they are for the benefit of those who do not know how to worship God for themselves, the Lord takes note of them, he pays attention to them.

He does not take them lightly, but takes them in the power, and authority by which they were released into the atmosphere, to flow up before his throne.

Our prayers serve God and help all God has destined for them to help by our faith, and belief in him, and our faith activates our prayers in front of the Lord.

There are people out in the world who pray, but because of the sinful life they live their prayers go unheard, and so a righteous prayer must be sent up for them.

And if we are unforgiving, then it may hinder the prayer God needs us to send up in front of his throne for the benefit of the one we refuse to forgive.

We can't afford to cast our spiritual life to the wind because our flesh refuses to be forgiving; it is all about God, and not about ourselves.

BRIDLING THE TONGUE

Words can build up or they can tear down, words can bring out the positivity in a person or they can bring anger, and hatred. Our words can be life giving or we can kill with one nasty word.

Our words can have the power of heaven or the eternal wrath of hell. Our words can express our inner most heartfelt love, and life; it is all according to the words we choose to use to express our thoughts, and what is in our hearts.

Words can take us on a journey when we read a book, or if we choose not to speak at all, without them we are quiet, and peaceful.

Words are a major part of our lives, and we all use them in our daily lives, people every day get hurt by an unkind word spoken at the most inappropriate times, and sometimes a bad word spoken when someone has had a bad day can cause a reaction that really was not wanted.

(Ja. 1:26) If anyone who is among you seems to look religious, and does not hold back his tongue, he is lying to his own heart, and this person's religion is senseless, and foolish.

Should any man who is among you, who seems to be devout, and does not curb his tongue, but misleads his own heart, you should expect this man's religion to be of no use.

Even though every man who is associated with you may appear to be faithful, and godly, at the same time there are those who do not control their tongues, but they mislead themselves, their devotion is egotistical, and fruitless, and only shows how their concern is about their own appearance, and not the things of God nor the body of Christ.

(Ja. 3:1) My brothers do not be to many teacher's know that we will suffer extreme accusations.

My brothers do not try to be a teacher of to many people, because you should know that you will have to endure a great degree of criticism.

(Ja. 3:2) Consider that in many things we are able to cause pain to all people. But should any man not hurt anyone with their words, this man is an excellent man, because he has the necessary power to restrain his whole body.

Because in many things we can cause pain to all people, but if any man doesn't cause pain through his word's this man is an excellent man, who is able to curb the desires of his entire body.

My experience is that in many matters we can hurt and anger all people, even so every man should refuse to hurt anyone with their words, in the way that Jesus Christ did.

And should he do as Jesus did, he is a man who is the same as Jesus Christ, having exceptional intelligence, and this person will show the same skills, talents, power, and authority that the Lord had in restraining and ruling over the entire body that he lived in.

(Ja. 3:5) Still the tongue is a small piece, and it boasts about big things. Look, how big a thing a small fire can kindle!

The tongue is a very small part of the body, and it can speak vain, exaggerations, and make them sound like they are bigger than they are. And this small part is able to work up (kindle) a rage (fire) in people!

(Ja. 3:6) And the tongue is a fire, a world of sin: so is the tongue amongst our components, that it defiles the entire body, and sets on fire the course of nature; and it is set on fire of hell.

And the tongue is a blaze, it is a world of sin; thus, is the tongue among our parts, it dirties the whole body, and sets a blaze in the progression of man's character; and it is set ablaze because it is connected to hell.

When this says "the tongue sets a blaze in the progression of a man's character", it is saying that the tongue can put a destructive personality into a man, that will either stop a man from growing spiritually or it will hinder the spiritual growth of the man by making sure it is delayed and unable to grow.

When the tongue is not being controlled by the Holy Spirit it will speak things that will ignite the fires of hell. The tongue of one who is not in Christ is an instrument of hell fire, it carries worldly ungodliness in it, and this is what the tongue can do as part of our physical bodies.

The tongue is also able to make our bodies dirty because of the nasty things it is able to say when it is not under control. It is able to take a man in the wrong direction, causing the man's character to burn in the fires of hell.

(Ja. 3:8) But the tongue no man can control; it is an uncontrollable evil, that is filled up with deadly poison.

The tongue no man can get under control; it is a disobedient wickedness; that is full of corruption and lethal venom.

The corruption and the venom that the tongue is full of

is malice, spitefulness, hatred, bitterness, and pretension, and so many other sinful emotions.

(Ja. 3:17) But the wise knowledge that comes from above is first true, and then peaceful, kind, and easy to be asked of, and is filled up with compassion and good fruits, he doesn't have any bias in him, and he is not a hypocrite.

But the informed knowledge that comes from the heaven's is first real, and then it is full of peace, and kindness, and it is not difficult to ask anything of, and it is full of love, and produces righteousness, and he has no bigotry in him, and he is no deceiver.

The knowledge that comes from God is first free from moral corruption: it avoids hostility, and is peaceful, kind, and merciful. It is not difficult to ask anything of, it is completely full of love, and righteous results.

It is not prejudice, and it is not pretentious. Pretension is a false showing of something; it is like wearing a mask or a veil, and every action that is done is fake, the person presents themselves to be righteous in character when they are not.

(Rev. 2:16) You are to apologize; and if you won't, I am going to come to you very fast, and I am going to fight against them, using the blade of my mouth.

We are to say we are sorry when we do something that is offensive, and if we do not then the LORD will come swiftly, and take action against those who were wrong, he will fight them, and he will do this using the sharpness (blade) of the Holy Spirit which is the power that he speaks with.

We carry the same sharpness (sword) that Jesus carries, in the power of our tongues, this sharpness and power is the spirit of the living God.

And in order to use it according to the will of God we have to stay under him in humility, so he can help us use his sword in the correct way he intended for it to be used.

Humility is the only way, and if a day comes when we are no longer humble, then that will be the day when we will no longer be allowed to use it.

Because flesh, and blood can't use it, and it will not be used outside of the humility that God says is needed to use it.

We as human beings who are sinful, our tongues are filled with venom, or you can say it is a deadly poison because of its connection to hell. But because of who Jesus is what comes out of his mouth is not poisonous or venomous, but it is a sharp spiritual blade that is made by the Holy Spirit, that helps us fight against the venom of the tongue when it is directed at us.

Also, Jesus teaches us about humility, being quiet, and being still while carrying this sword, one of the reason's he insists on this is because when you are quiet, and you open your mouth at his appointed time it makes more of an impact then it would if you did not learn how to control your tongue.

See with the tongue it is all about power; power to change, power to redirect, and the power to make a difference, when guided by the Holy Spirit.

HOLY GROUND

Moses went to talk to God on his mountain that was called mount Horeb: when he got there, he had to take his shoes off before he stepped onto that land to talk with God, because they represented the flesh of man, and flesh could not enter into God's land.

When he did as God told him to, taking the shoes off, he took off the fleshly man, and he showed his obedience by humbling himself before God, leaving behind the representation of the old man that was of the flesh, and taking on the new man of God that he was to become.

He readied himself to go do the will of the Lord, and the will of the Lord was for him to go and deliver his people Israel out of the hand of bondage to the Egyptians.

(Ex. 3:4) And at the time the LORD saw he turned towards his direction to see, God called to him out of the middle of the bush, and said Moses, Moses, and he said, I am Here.

Then at the moment the LORD was able to see Moses turning to come into his direction to see the bush that was burning, then God called out to him from the center of the bush, and said Moses, Moses, and Moses said here I am.

God was the reason that Moses moved in his direction, bringing him to his mountain; because the Spirit of God drew him, and then the spirit touched him, and then his spirit pulled on Moses and made him come to him.

(Ex. 3:5) Then he said, Do not come any closer to this place: take your shoes off of your feet, because the place whereupon you are standing is holy ground.

God told him his shoes had to come off, and that he could not walk onto Holy Ground wearing those shoes. When he came to see him, he had to be given the shoes God had made for him.

He also could not walk onto Holy Ground wearing those shoes because those shoes where the shoes of the man Moses was before he answered God's call.

When he let those shoes go, and he stepped onto Holy Ground God raised him up into the spiritual realm and put the spiritual man on him.

Then he became the man of God the Lord called him to be, putting down his flesh, and the shoes that represented it, and putting on the shoes that were governed by the supernatural governor of God, Jesus Christ.

He would not let him come any closer until Moses took those shoes off of his feet, and until he took them off, he could not come any closer to God than God would allow him to, until he obeyed him, and took those shoes off, and left them on the earth were they came from.

He wanted them left right where Moses was standing so God could set him to the duty, he had called him to do, God wanted to put a new pair of shoes on Moses; he wanted to put the shoes of peace on him, the shoes that were only provided by God.

When one puts off the shoes of the flesh, they put off the sin, and the hostility that comes with them, and when one yields to the will of the Lord he replaces those earthly shoes with the shoes of peace, that are the Holy Spirit of God. God knew Moses was going to have to endure in what he knew he was sending him to do, and he knew Moses was going to have to suffer for the task he knew was at hand for him.

God not only set Moses apart for his own purposes, but he also arranged Moses life so that he would finally be put in the proper hands of God so he could be ordered to do what God needed him to do.

So, God could finally give him the responsibility to get the work done. When God said the word whereupon, he was asking Moses do you know on what place you have come to? He asked him did he know where he was, and did he know what he was facing? Then he told him the place you have come onto is consecrated, and Holy Ground.

This place gets its sanctification directly from me because it's connected to me, and it is connected to me because I am dwelling in it right now, I am present on it, and my presences is what makes this place Holy Ground.

When you step onto this ground you will be stepping onto Higher Ground. It is Higher Ground because when you stepped onto it you were stepping in, and up into the spiritual elevations of where I dwell to talk with me on a higher spiritual plain. I will elevate you to your chosen position, and I will change you into the higher spiritual being I have called you to be.

Do not try to step onto Holy Ground if you are not ready to be placed on Higher Ground. If you are not ready to face the true work God has for you to do, once you step onto it you can't turn back, you belong to God.

You can't be placed onto Higher Ground if you do not step onto Holy Ground and come in the way God has told you to come, taking the shoes off of your feet, and in doing so taking off the flesh that will hinder you, and the flesh that is not welcome to walk onto Gods Holy Ground.

(Josh. 5:15) And the captain of the LORD's army said to Joshua, release your shoe's, and take them off of your feet; because the place where you are standing is holy. And Joshua did what he was asked.

A leader of the LORD's army said to Joshua, take your shoes off; because this place is sacred, and you are standing on it. So, Joshua did what he was directed to do. Joshua like Moses took the shoes off of his feet because he also came to understand that he was standing on Higher Ground.

(Ps. 37:23) The footsteps of a righteous man are arranged by the LORD: and he delights in his direction.

The footsteps that a righteous man takes, the LORD is the one who arranges them, looking after the man, and guiding him in the direction he is to go, and while he is doing this, he is delighted in the way the man is walking, because the LORD knows he is moving in the way that he wants him to, walking on higher ground.

FAITH

The other day I woke up, and I heard "faith is the substance of things hoped for, the evidence of things not seen."

(Heb. 11:1) At this time faith is the consistent thing that we hope for and is the proof of the things we cannot see.

Now faith is the principle of things that we look forward to, and the proof of things that we aren't able to see.

At this moment belief lives, belief is the reason that belief continues, belief is the real proof of the reality of God. It is the evidence of God; it is the proof of his real existence, and the reason for his way of thinking.

And when I opened a letter my brother in Christ sent me, he was talking about faith with works too. That was so precious to see coming from him, and to me he said I have to not give up hope, and neither would he. One can't have faith, and not have works, our faith is our works, and love, and being able to love are part of our faith.

Faith is something that should steadily grow because it is true, and real, and we should stick together in it. And we should constantly hope for it.

Faith serves as evidence of the things we are unable to see, that are of the God we are unable to see with our natural eyes. Our faith is proof that there is a real God in the heaven's that the eyes of the flesh can't see, but by our faith we know that he does live.

We are supposed to look forward to the essential nature of God with desire, like it is something to be experienced, belief is the proof that the thoughts of the unseen God do live.

In having faith, we acknowledge to God that we believe he is real, and to him faith is the proof that we know he lives. Faith is proof that we belong to Him, and only one who truly belongs to him is able to have faith in him.

Our walk through this life in Gods faith is our proving ground to God that proves that we truly love him, anyone not walking by faith, and claiming to know him their walk and their works will prove them.

And it really does not matter if they are proven in front of men, all that matters is that they will be revealed in time by God.

We as the children of God just have to have faith, and believe in him, and remember that no matter how long he allows us to be in a situation or to sit in certain places he will answer no matter how long it takes, he will answer.

He never leaves us nor forsakes us; he is always by our side; he never forgets his children.

The word forsake means to abandon, and he will not do to us what we do not do to him. He wants us to remember him, and not leave him; we have to trust him, and believe in him, and have faith in him.

He has kept us this long, and he will continue to keep us, we are not to lose heart, and are to be at peace on the inside, especially during the trials that come to try us, and that try to overtake us.

(Isa. 41:17) At this time those who are in poverty and in need looked for water; and there was none, their tongues were useless because it was craving water, I the LORD will hear them, and I the God of Israel will not leave them.

When those who are weak, and those who are in need search for water, and there is none to be found, their tongues are of no use because their tongues need water, and I the LORD will hear them, and I the God of Israel will not give up on them.

These people who have nothing, and who are destitute, they are so because they are unable to find God's living water, so they spiritually have nothing and are lacking something important.

And in the places that they are looking they can't find anything spiritually, and they are unable to quench the thirst that is in their souls. What they were lacking that was important was God's spiritual water.

Their tongues do not desire water of the earth, they desire spiritual water that is the word of God, and earthly water could never quench their thirst. The only water that could ever quench their thirst is the water only God can provide.

As the Lord is sitting on his throne, that he will do, and he makes the choice according to his will, and his many mercies, to pay attention to them, and listen to them, and will not quite on them, and he certainly has no intention of leaving them.

Because in spite of the fact at the time they have been unable to find what they are looking for, they still continued to search for him, and his holy water. They were faithful to him, and he was determined to be faithful to them.

In their continuing to search for what their tongues wanted, and though their road was made very hard they were determined, and they continued to search for God, God saw this, and did not forget them, they had great faith.

DO YOU KNOW WHO YOU ARE? PRAYER

Do you know who you are? I know who you are, so let me tell you who you are! You are the righteousness of God! You are one of the upright in God who walks in goodness, in Godly innocence, and Godly righteousness, you are a child of the king.

(1 Pe. 2:5) You as well, like living stones, happen to be a put together spiritual house, and a holy priesthood, and the reason for this is so you can offer up spiritual offerings, that are pleasing to God being able to do this through Jesus Christ.

You are considered to be stones that are full of life, that happen to be a built-up spiritual body of believers (house), and a godly priesthood, to give up spiritual offerings, that are satisfying to God through Jesus Christ.

My beloved brother you are a child of the Most High God, you are part of a royal priesthood, you are a piece of the descendants that come from the linage of King Jesus, who come through the office of the priesthood.

A part of Gods' holy nation, a vessel of honor, you are one of those who are devoted to his service, and we are to let it be known through the praises that we give to him that we are those who were called by him to come out of the darkness of sin into his marvelous light of righteousness:

This verse says we come from a line of royal priests, it

did not say we came from a line of prophet's, or a line of disciples or even a line of Apostles, it said we came from a royal priesthood.

And Jesus is a royal priest, and we are made like him. I am not saying that God does not have the right to call any of us prophet's or disciples even Apostles, he will call us what he will call us, but this is the line that the word says we come from, a royal priesthood.

(1 Pe. 2:9) But you are a selected generation, a dignified priesthood, a holy nation, an unusual people; so, you should show from the praises of him who has called you out of the darkness into his incredible light:

But you are a chosen generation, a royal priesthood, a specially dedicated tribe, an uncommon people; because of this you ought to show this when you praise him, because he is the one who has summoned you to come out of the darkness into his glorious light:

(2 Tim. 2:20) But in a decent house there's not only pots made of gold and silver, but there's also pot's that are made of wood and dirt, and some of these pots are honorable, and some pots have no honor.

This verse is saying that in the house of God there are gold and silver vessels, these vessels are people of honor, who are not living sinful lives. The vessels that are made of wood and dirt are people who are full of sin, earthly people, and when it says that in a decent house these vessels are there together it is saying that his children have to grow spiritually in the church with the children who are sinful, and who are the children of Satan.

(2 Tim. 2:21) If a man then cleans himself from these,

he will be a vessel to honor, cleaned up and shown to be put in place for the master's use, and made ready to all righteous work.

If a man cleans himself up from sin, he will become a person who is full of honor, and then he will be put in a position to do the Lord's work, he will do this because God would have made him ready to do his holy work.

We are the offspring of Jesus Christ, and since his death on the cross we have been called to carry his testimony to all who are in the earth, we are his legacy, and his heirs.

(Rom. 4:13) Because the promise, in order that he would be the heir of the world, was not just given to Abraham, or to his seed, through the law, but it was through the sacredness of faith.

This promise was made to Abraham so he could become the heir of the world, and the promise that God made to Abraham was not just made to him, it was also made to his descendants.

And it was not made through the law of Moses, it was made through the holiness of faith, the faith that his children would have in him down through the generations.

(Ex. 19:5) At this time then, if you will truly obey my voice, and keep my covenant, then you will be a peculiar treasure to me above all people: because all the earth is mine:

Now, if you will really be obedient to my voice, and carry out my agreement, then you will be an unusual treasure to me over all people: because everything in the earth is mine:

(Matt. 24:21) Because then will be immense troubles, like there never was since the beginning of the world till this time, nor ever will be again.

There will be immeasurable troubles, and they are troubles that had not been seen since the world was first made, and these troubles would never happen again.

(Matt. 24:22) And unless those days would be made shorter, there would be no one in the flesh to be set free: however, for the chosen's benefit those days will be shortened.

These days would have to be shortened, because if they were not then no person would have been able to be redeemed, and for the chosen children of God's benefit those days were going to be shortened.

These were the troubled times that were to come that would happen during the time of Jesus Christ death, burial, and resurrection.

(Matt. 24:31) And he will send his angels out with a mighty sound of a trumpet, and they will bring together his chosen from the four corners of the heavens, from one end of heaven to the other.

God will send his angels out when they hear the powerful sound of his trumpet, and they will gather together God's children from the distant parts of the earth, this is what the four corners of the heavens means, from one end of the earth to the other.

(Matt. 5:14) You are the light of the world. A city who is set up on a hill is unable to be hidden.

We are lights, and are beacons, to be seen by the whole world, like the beacon that shines from a light house for all the ships in the harbor to see so they will not hit the rocks or run up on dry land.

The beacon the ships sail by is a warning beacon, and that is what we are, lights of warning God has place in the earth to warn man of his presence. And because of the fact that we are warning lights we can't be hidden, because our lights shine so bright.

The Prophet's in the Old Testament were warning lights too, who had been placed in the earth to warn man of his presence as well. They spoke for him amongst men, they would warn people, they were sent to by God to tell men of things he needed them to known.

(Isa. 35:10) And the redeemed of the LORD will come back and come to Zion singing songs and having a joy on their minds that will last forever: they will attain joy and gladness; sorrow and sighing will flee from them.

The redeemed of the LORD will return to him, and when they do, they will go to Zion singing songs, and joy will be in their minds.

And this joy will never end, lasting for all eternity, and they will come to have joy, and gladness, and grief and sighing will run away from them.

We are the redeemed of the LORD, that he rescued from the punishment of sin by his death on the cross, when he paid redemption's price.

And by paying it he redeemed us from being in captivity to Satan and sin. With his death on the cross he paid the ransom price for us, and this made us the redeemed of the Lord.

To me this is who we are, our lives before Jesus Christ does not matter to God, and after Jesus Christ our sins are forgiven, and remembered no more: that is just the way it is.

(Ps. 111:10) When the LORD is feared it is the beginning of coming to know wisdom: a good awareness all have who do his commandments: his praises endure forever.

The beginning of coming to know wisdom starts with being in awe of the LORD, this is what fearing him means, excellent knowledge is what all the children will have who follow the LORD's commands: his praises will last forever.

We will praise him for all eternity, and through us doing this through the years his praises will continue forever.

To find wisdom is to find knowledge of what is right and true, and to be able to have just judgment, being able to have clear understanding, and spiritual insight, that comes from the God of wisdom.

When one receives wisdom, they are able to speak wise things, they are able to teach wisdom, and they will have wise habits.

The word fear in this sentence means reverence, when we begin to reverence him, and finally see he is an awesome God we will begin to show him the respect he deserves.

And when we begin to do that then it is the first steps to being enlightened, and the first steps in starting to cooperate with him, and once we begin to cooperate with him then we begin to learn how to be familiar with him.

Then we begin to slowly embrace him, and then we begin to take in his knowledge, we come to an understanding of him, and who we are.

We begin to learn from him, and we learn how to rightly divide the word, and how to speak the word. We also have to learn how to hold onto everything that God teaches us, holding them in our hearts, and keeping them in our minds.

The Lord burns his word into our hearts and minds as well, and what this means is he plants the word in our hearts, and minds, using the Holy Ghost to do this work.

And after the Holy Ghost is placed in us it begins to grow and then it causes us to grow in the spiritual realm, and as it grows it begins to speak to us, and speak through us, and eventually speaks for us.

It takes over every communication for us to the Father, and comes alive in our lives, slowly and surely.

Here is some advice should you choose to seek out the LORD, make the dictionary a companion to the bible when studying the word, it has helped me learn a lot, and it taught me God can use anything to teach his children wisdom. As you get in the word and begin to learn, the more you become who God has intended for you to be.

The word transforms you, changing you and causing you to become a different person, and the person you once were you are no longer.

You become a new creation in Christ, and remember to pray, prayer changes things, prayer opens doors, and prayer is a direct connection to God, prayer is the communion that God wants us to have with him.

Also, our prayers flow into his nose, along with his fragrant incenses, these prayers, and incenses are precious to him, and they smell good to him, this is how he takes in our prayers.

Our prayers assist the right, and just children of God in getting their prayers to his throne to be heard, our prayers serve us, and they serve God. They serve us because they are a powerful force, and they are very efficient when we desire something of the almighty.

And they serve him in being the help we send before him when we need, and want his power, and great assistance in what is going on in our lives.

And also remember no matter how long it takes God to come, and answer your prayers, you are never forgotten, he keeps account of all his children.

Every hair on our heads are counted, and every tear is placed before the throne of God as a gift of remembrance of us, and who we are to him, and to show we have need of him, he desires us to need him.

(Matt. 10:30) Yet the actual hairs of your heads are all counted.

No man on earth can declare true son ship when it comes to being a son of God, though many have tried, but it is the Father who declares our son ship. No man can make this possible nor can they truly declare it to be so.

What declares us to have true son ship is when we follow the true principles laid down by the Father, and his son Jesus Christ, and one of his primary authentic principles, is prayer.

When it came to prayer Jesus entered into it, and he entered into it often, sometimes he spent all night in prayer, he spent all night in prayer because the night was darkness.

And he needed to pray most during the darkness, the darkness is the time when men can't see, and God also dwells in the darkness, so he brings us the light out of the darkness.

And after hearing from the Father, he spoke only what he heard of the Father, the Father enlightened him with his word, and his instructions, he guided Jesus.

In prayer he saw his Father doing many miraculous, and marvelous things, and after witnessing his Father's business he did as his Father did.

God's house of prayer, his temple is not a building made by man's hands out of wood or stone, but is made by Jesus Christ, and is made of living stones who are the children of the Most High God, who are joined together into his corporate body.

We are to be praying stones who make up the house of prayer. Real prayer does not come from self, and it does not come from carnal minded worship from a carnal mind, or selfish desires, but true prayer is born out of sorrow, and then these sorrows are raised up into a glorified praise.

This prayer is prompted by the darkness of night, but God raises it into a praise of glory, a prayer that starts in sorrow, in the inner man, and ends in glory, victory, and praising the Lord.

Worship is a pouring out of one's soul to God having the mind set of giving rather than receiving. Great hardship, and sorrow releases an outpouring in prayer that is heard by the Father as it rises to his throne, our deliverance coming 1st in heaven, then on the earth.

JUDGE NOT

(Matt. 7:1) Do not judge anyone, so you will not be judged.

Do not be critical of others, do not decide on your own to give an unneeded opinion of another person, do not take up that place, so God will not be a judge over you.

(Matt. 7:2) Because with what judgment you judge, you will be judged: and with what method you deal out, it will be the method that is given to you in return, at a later time.

Because of the true nature of the real judge Jesus Christ there will be sever judgment, and you should expect the Lords official evaluation: and because of the true nature of that part of you that sins.

That chose to deal out what you did, you should expect a fair share of what you dealt out to be given back to you at some time in the future, because of the choice that you made.

(Matt. 7:3) And why do you behold the fragment in your brother's eye, but do not consider the fragment in your own eye?

For what reason do you see the small fault (fragment), that blocks your brother's eye, yet you pay no attention to the fault that is in your own eye?

(Matt. 7:4) Or how will you say to your brother, let me take the fragment out of your eye; and look a fragment is in your own eye?

Otherwise for what reason do you choose to say to your brother, allow me to remove the small fault out of your eye, so I can uncover what is in your eye, do you see the fault in your own eye?

(Matt. 7:5) You are an impostor, first you have to remove the flaw out of your own eye; then will you be able to see clearly to help your brother remove the fragment out of his eyes.

You are a liar, for the first time throw away the fault's you have in your own eye; then you will come to know that without a doubt you will be able to help get rid of the faults in your brother's eyes, and then you will be able to bring this problem to a final conclusion.

These verses remind us about what not to do when it comes to judging someone, I do not want to be judged for anything I might knowingly judge someone else for, and when we judge we may see our judging in one way, but God knows the heart.

And he knows how a man's heart is really judging at the time it judges someone. We may think we are not even judging someone at the time that we are, but God knows what we are doing at all times.

When one judges they have something inside of themselves that is sinful, and they need to ask God to deal with it. So, if one is in this state of mind how can they judge someone else for the wrongs they believe that person is doing?

They have to get what is wrong inside of themselves out before they can help another person remove what is inside of them that's wrong. It is considered being a hypocrite to judge someone else for the wrongs in their life when your life is just as messed up.

(Lk. 6:37) Do not judge, and you will not be judged: do

not condemn, and you will not be condemned: forgive, and you will be forgiven:

Do not be critical, and then you will not be criticized: count no one to be unfit for Gods use, and do not expect to be counted for Gods use, pardon for any wrongs done to you, and God will pardon you for any wrongs you may have done to someone else.

(Lk. 6:38) Give, and it will be given to you; good amounts will be measured out, compressed down, and thoroughly examined, and always, men will give into your being. Because with the same measures that you measure out as well it will be measured back to you again.

Voluntarily give, and do not expect anything in return, and then you can look forward to things being given to you. God will present you with gifts that he will place on the inside of you, and these gifts will make you have life, and they will bloom in your life.

If we give real, and trustworthy parts of ourselves, God will make good works come to those who are giving, and actions come to those he loves.

These would come from the hand of those who would oppose him, and they will oppose Jesus in their work with a steadily applied force, this would be done to put a heavy weight on us while God watches from his throne.

This would cause us to be forced into our exalted positions, and it will make us humble through the descending pressures of what we must go through for Christ sake.

At the same time being under the weight of the pressure, it can cause us to tremble, and shake because of the emotional being that we are on the inside.

This pressure could cause instability, and disorders in our lives had we not been following Jesus, still this is the walk we must take.

This happens to all of God's children, and it happens at the same time, jointly, causing us to take flight above in the spiritual realm of the heavens. We are to expect this because of what men do to us, and because of this God is using them to definitely impart to the inside of us what we need.

Going through these hard times makes us humble, and kind, and this makes the Father, and the Son embrace us.

In order to obtain this, we are to give with all hope knowing that this is going to happen; the part that you give is a part of you, and it will return to you.

When we give from our hearts God blesses us greatly, but when we are selfish, he punishes us greatly too. I do not want the reward's that come with being selfish and judging other's; I want to be rewarded with the good, and perfect things God has, and wants to give to me.

People who judge, and condemn others really have no life of their own, they are too used to living in other people's business. And are usually very ignorant to their own faults, and imperfections.

They do not see their own because they are too busy looking at everybody else's, blaming, and pointing fingers at others, and talking about other people's faults, they have imagined them to have, anything to keep the focus off of themselves.

How Jesus sums up a man's life is totally different than how man does; man seldom holds any value on a human life which happens to be the soul of a man.

Man's value has always been what they could get for the services of the human flesh. Services like slavery, prostitution, and even the salaries people are paid today for their work.

God on the other hand values the soul of a man, he sums up a man not by what he has done in his flesh, but by what he has given from his heart. He does not judge the prostitute for selling her body, he loves her.

And he loves her until she learns how to love herself, and she learns how to love herself by learning about Jesus undying love for her. And the beginning of her love for herself is when she turns her life over to Christ for when she does that, she is saying she loves Jesus, and she wants Jesus to love her back.

Look, Mary Magdalene was considered to be a sinner, and Jesus forgave her, and told her to go, and sin no more.

(Lk. 7:37) And look, a woman in the city, that was a sinner, at the time she knew that Jesus was sitting at a meal in the Pharisee's home, brought in an alabaster box that had ointment in it,

See, there was a woman who was sinful, and she was in the city, and at this time she knew Jesus was sitting down to have dinner in the home of a Pharisee, when she came into the house, she brought an alabaster box in with her that had ointment in it,

(Lk. 7:38) And she stood at his feet, standing behind him crying, and started to wash his feet with her tears, then she wiped them with hair from her head, then she kissed them, then she anointed them with the ointment.

When she went in the house she stood at Jesus feet, she was standing behind him crying, then she began to clean his feet with her tears and wipe them off with the hair from her head, and then she kissed them, and then she rubbed the ointment on them.

(Lk. 7:47) And because of this, I am saying to you, Her sins that are many, are forgiven, those who are like her only love very little.

Jesus said, and because of what she has done, I am saying to you, that though her sins are many, they are forgiven, because people who are like her simply put, show very little love.

(Lk. 48) Then he said to her, your sins are forgiven.

Then he told her, your sins have been forgiven.

God told me not to judge my friend, and all I needed to know was that he belonged to God, so I chose to speak of him from my heart, in the truth of God.

And no matter what anyone said I would not line up against him because of what man said, what man says does not matter to God, and it did not matter to me, if I judged him, I would have rather judged him with the righteousness of God and say from my heart he is a son of God.

And a partaker with all the other heirs, and joint heirs in Jesus Christ that is who he is. I know this is who he is because God told me this was who he was, and God does not lie.

If we forgive anyone their sins, they are forgiven: if we do not forgive them, they are not forgiven by us, but they always have the opportunity to be forgiven by God.

But if we do not forgive, then we are not being obedient to the will of the Lord, and we ourselves will be facing judgment at the Lord's hands.

Anyway, how can we say that we believe in the Lord, and his word and not be forgiving, that would mean that we are not following him in the way he wants us to, and only his children honor his word, and what he asks them to do.

And his word says that those who rebel against him are none of his, so his children do not go against his will, and what he wants for us, the Holy Spirit makes sure we don't, it would never turn on the Father, and the son.

www.ingramcontent.com/pod-product-compliance
Lightning Source LLC
Chambersburg PA
CBHW071326110526
44591CB00010B/1035